AMERICA THE WRONG WAY

On the trail of a nation's soul

Chris Harris

Bloomington, IN

authorHOUSE™

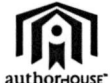

Milton Keynes, UK

AuthorHouse™
1663 Liberty Drive, Suite 200
Bloomington, IN 47403
www.authorhouse.com
Phone: 1-800-839-8640

AuthorHouse™ UK Ltd.
500 Avebury Boulevard
Central Milton Keynes, MK9 2BE
www.authorhouse.co.uk
Phone: 08001974150

© 2006 Chris Harris. All Rights Reserved.

No part of this book may be reproduced, stored in a retrieval system, or transmitted by any means without the written permission of the author.

First published by AuthorHouse 01/26/06

ISBN: 1-4259-0940-X (sc)

Printed in the United States of America
Bloomington, Indiana

This book is printed on acid-free paper.

America the Wrong Way

'America the Wrong Way' is not an insightful exposé of the Bush-Schwarzenegger Texas-Hollywood axis, nor is it a critique of the might of the Military-Industrial-Globalisation complex. It is a light-hearted account of a coast-to-coast journey across America in a west to east direction, attempting to follow the historic Route 66 for much of the way and travelling in an old open-top gas guzzler. This story is not 'just another travelogue.' An anecdotal style highlights the beauty and warmth of America and its people, and tells the very human stories of people and places encountered en route. The foibles and idiosyncrasies of characters, and the tragedies and triumphs of American history, are seen through the perceptive but sympathetic eyes of a visitor from Europe.

This pathfinding journey was the warm-up act for an all-girl tribute band on the run, drawn from a troop of sprightly swingers the wrong side of sixty, as an unsuspecting America faced the biggest outbreak of trans-Atlantic musical mayhem since the Beatles hit New York's Shea Stadium in 1965.

'America the Wrong Way' was originally born out of a project to raise money for charity, and a contribution from the

net proceeds goes to support sufferers from Motor Neurone Disease.

Chris Harris is one of the select band of writers never to have been shortlisted for either the Booker Prize or the Nobel Prize for Literature. In real life he is a management consultant with an MBA from the Edinburgh Business School who lives and works in the east of England. '*America the Wrong Way*' is his first work to reach the bookstores of the high streets and the airport terminals. Some may say it is the only interesting thing he has ever written – he normally writes on such arcane topics as digital convergence and competitive strategies. His earlier works, which include 'Telecommunications across the Millennial Divide' and 'Wegomlegging – Three years in the Byways of Belgium', have become collectors' items for the discerning cognoscenti.

For Lois, my wife and co-pilot

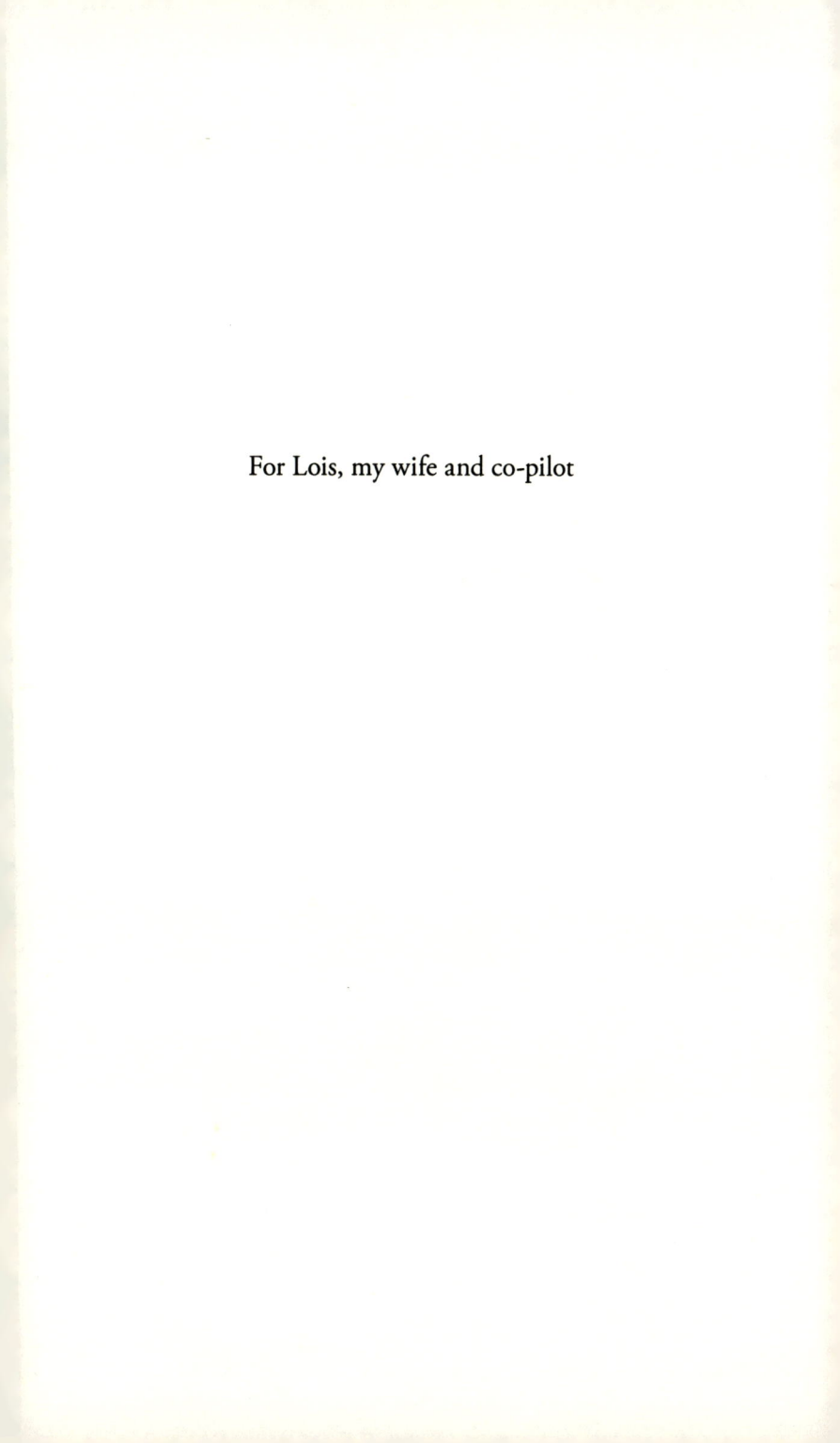

Chapter 1

As we stepped from San Francisco Airport's terminal building onto the sidewalk, our spirits were marvellously lifted by a welcoming wall of warmth, a luxuriant Californian greeting which embraced us after an air-conditioned flight from chilly London. In the crowded arrivals hall, we had vainly scanned the assembled throng of meeters and greeters, and it was somewhat wounding to our vanity to discover that Governor Schwarzenegger was not on hand to welcome us. What could possibly have gone wrong? I had definitely written to warn him we were coming. The most likely explanation seemed to be that some gubernatorial flunky had double booked Arnold's desk calendar.

It was a terminator from a different continent and an earlier age who memorably said, "A journey of a thousand miles starts with a single step." The first small step on this epic journey across America was taken months earlier with an offer to help a friend, casually made on the spur of the moment.

Our good friend Andrew had been talking about his vision (or crazy scheme, depending on your point of view) of driving across America to raise money for a British charity with which he and his wife Christine were closely linked. The charity was committed to providing support to local sufferers of Motor Neurone Disease (MND), or Amyotrophic Lateral Sclerosis (ALS) as it is generally known in the USA, a distressing degenerative condition for which there is no known prevention or cure, from which Christine's mum Lorna, who had passed away the previous year, had suffered.

Lorna had been an accomplished and enthusiastic pianist, and a leading light in a group of entertainers calling themselves the Silver Minstrels. She was a lady who loved life. Surviving members of Lorna's team, now a troop of sprightly swingers the wrong side of sixty, were keen to join the trek as an all-girl tribute band on the run. An unsuspecting America was faced with the biggest outbreak of trans-Atlantic musical mayhem since the Beatles hit New York's Shea Stadium in 1965. The general aim of the project would be to drive the historic Route 66 from the shores of Lake Michigan in Chicago to the Pacific Ocean at Santa Monica in a period vehicle, to raise as much cash as possible through sponsorships and by giving impromptu concerts along the route, and to have some fun in the process.

Andrew was determined to make the journey in style in a classic American car, ideally a 1950s Cadillac convertible with all the sweeping tails and fins and ostentation of the era. But the project bristled with uncertainties and with logistical challenges. Would it be outlandishly expensive to buy such a vehicle? Could one be rented? Or better still, was there a generous and trusting benefactor out there, a kindly soul who would be rash enough to lend his or her precious Caddy? Did the project make financial sense as a charitable fund raising venture? Where could a suitable vehicle be found for sale? Andrew was several thousand miles away in

England, so who would purchase it and who would prepare it for action? Would it be possible for a team of foreigners to take out insurance on it? Would an old vehicle stand up to the mechanical rigours of such a long journey? Like so many other wacky ideas, it was clear that this was destined to remain a pipedream!

But visions aren't that easily dispelled. Ebay listings were scanned, and internet search engines began churning over the keywords; Cadillac, used vehicles, fifties, sixties, convertible. Preliminary research results indicated that a pristine Caddy of that vintage would cost a small fortune to buy, and that one certainly couldn't be rented or borrowed. The same research indicated that, if a suitable car could be found, the most likely source would be sunny California. Quite understandably, more open top touring cars had been sold in that state than in any other, and the hot dry climate of southern California had contributed to their survival in working order. In other states, where snow, ice and salted roads were regular winter conditions, rust had long since taken its toll and consigned most of these gas guzzling veterans to wreckers' yards. This presented an obvious logistical issue before Andrew's expedition could even start. How would this vehicle get from California to Chicago, which was the beginning of Route 66 and the starting point of Andrew's project?

"We'd be very happy to fly out to California and drive the vehicle across America in the opposite direction, if that would be any help," I offered, without so much as a single word of consultation with my co-driver, navigator and wife, Lois. Hey, it sounded like a fun trip! The glamour, the romance, the sunshine, the open top motoring, the freedom of the open road and the wide horizons of the great American west. But of course, it would never happen.

The offer was quickly made and soon forgotten, but not by Andrew who stored it away for future reference. When a suitable vehicle was eventually located and purchased, it wasn't exactly a 1950s Caddy; it was a 1974 Pontiac Grande Ville convertible, almost two tons of shiny blue and white open-top touring car with all the chrome and ostentation of a bygone era. And yes, it was waiting for us in California, at Sacramento. We were committed and there was no going back. And that, in a nutshell, is how it all began.

Like many others, I had long harboured an undeclared ambition to drive across America. After all, it was eminently achievable and sounded exciting, and it could all be done in the upholstered comfort of a car, with the prospect of a cosy motel room at the end of each day. Unlike trekking to either the North or the South Pole, it didn't involve the risks of either starving or freezing to death! And it was unlikely to involve tents, mountains, white water, wild beasts or bandits. It was the kind of adventure suitable for softies. Yet for twenty first century softies, driving America coast to coast still satisfied a primitive desire to be an explorer. It appealed to a sense of history, re-enacting the adventure of the pioneer settlers of yore and promising an eclectic blend of destinations, both the well-known and the unknown. And it involved a challenge that was way outside of the traditional British comfort zone of package and fly-drive.

I'd mulled over the route I would take. My preferred itinerary was a meandering northerly trajectory through the badlands of Dakota, stopping off to admire the Presidential features at the Mount Rushmore National Park, admiring the grandeurs of Wyoming's Yellowstone and Grand Teton National Parks, traversing the mighty Rockies, breaching the rugged Sierra Nevada by the Tioga Pass into fabled Yosemite, and drifting down the old gold-mining trail of the forty-niners into San Francisco. Or possibly a southern route would be better, hitting the trail from Miami, threading through the old deep south of Alabama and Louisiana, crossing Texas and the southern deserts, and slipping into Los Angeles via Phoenix and Palm Springs.

But whichever route was to be taken, it would definitely be from east to west. The 'going west' psychology was strongly ingrained. Whoever it was who first said "Go west, young man!" was both following an old pattern and establishing a new trend. Move from the old world to the new. Follow the sun, pursue your dreams, reach for the sky. The sunshine state was everyone's destination. The Pacific Ocean was the target.

So it seemed to be totally counter cultural to start our journey in California. It didn't feel quite right to make the journey from west to east, to cross America the wrong way. The psychology was all wrong, and so were the guide books, as all the routings we looked up were firmly described with an east to west presumption. And what was this about Route 66? I'd never heard of it! But apparently it was famous, and two generations had grown up with a romanticized notion of driving America's 'mother road', following the wavy concrete ribbon by which over the years many thousands had made the journey from middle America to the Pacific, either as migrants in the twenties and thirties, or as vacationers in the forties and fifties. Someone called Bobby Troup (never heard of him!) had immortalized it in the song,

> "If you ever plan to motor west
> Travel my way, take the highway that's the best
> Get your kicks on Route 66."

I listened to the song for the first and only time. The lyrics didn't grab me. It didn't scan. I didn't even like the tune.

Since those heady times, the historic Route 66 had apparently fallen on hard times. With the completion of the federal Interstate network of highways in the 1960s, the old route had been decommissioned as a national route. Small and isolated communities along the route had withered and died, motels and gasoline stations had closed. The 66 appellation had been removed and the route no longer appeared on maps. In many places the physical road itself had fallen into disrepair, in others it had been subsumed into local roads, in others it had disappeared under the fabric of the new Interstate highway. But in recent years a new nostalgia had taken root, and the old Route 66 was experiencing a rebirth. Local 'Route 66 Associations' were checking out the condition of the old road in their States. Rumours were around that there were signs of life in the old road yet. A few travellers were once again venturing out onto the 'mother road'. And we would be among them, but going the wrong way.

But all this enthusiasm for 'historic' Route 66 had totally passed me by. I was very familiar with Britain's A66, a spectacular undulating highway which crosses England from east to west, linking Scotch Corner on the Great North Road with Penrith south of the Scottish border. This historic A66 bisects the northern Pennines, the chain of limestone hills and high moors which forms the north-south backbone of England. It was built almost 2000 years ago as a highway for trade and for the imposition of military control by the occupying Romans, a people with a deep understanding of civil engineering and sewage systems. In AD 124, the enlisted men of the First Cohort of Tungrians garrisoning the Roman forts on Hadrian's Wall, wild hairy men from the tribes of the Belgae isolated on the far fringes of empire and assaulted by the driving rain of the high country and by hostile Pictish warriors, would have been anxiously scanning the A66 for signs of the next delivery of Belgian waffles and Leffe Blonde from far off home. In my book, that's real history!

But Route 66 was only created in 1926, and that didn't seem to me to be particularly historic. And why all this sentimental nostalgia for travelling a redundant road? I tried to imagine a parallel movement in England, with the 'Friends of the A5' promoting a romantic return to the historic transport cafés and lay-bys of the English Midlands, and re-enacting the march of the Roman Legions from Londinium and Verulamium to Deva to subdue troublesome tribes on the Welsh borders. Somehow it was difficult to visualise.

It was in this rather negative frame of mind that we sat down to view a video about Route 66. This was an important part of our orientation programme and mental preparation. In fact, apart from purchasing a slim book of maps, it was our only preparation. The video proved to be singularly discouraging. It appeared that we were destined to follow a nondescript highway, peopled by geriatric crones and verbally challenged anoraks who were living out a distant dream which we did not share. The scenic highlights were to be the largest car wrecker's yard in America, a red barn, a blue plastic whale and the home of the inventor of the hotdog on a stick. If the video was an accurate representation, Route 66 existed in a perpetual state of gloomy twilight. In several clips, the sensible travellers could be seen humming along the modern highway on the horizon in their modern cars. Our discouragement deepened. Was this really where we were going? We switched off the video half way through and made a decision. The less advance information we had, the better. We would wing it, and discover the secrets of Route 66 for ourselves.

And so it was that we left these shores, probably the most ill-prepared expedition since Franklin set out on his final voyage to discover the North West Passage over a hundred and fifty years before, or since Winnie-the-Pooh set out to find the East Pole. The days immediately prior to our departure had been filled with an intensive round of appointments and the comings and goings of builders and plumbers, activities which had jostled out most travel preparations. Every instinct told us that a couple of weeks of total inactivity on some sunny beach would suit us nicely. What we had in store hardly seemed recuperative.

But these momentary and unworthy instincts were given short shrift. Our immediate destination was San Francisco, our very favourite US city, a city which more than a decade before had been a regular monthly commuter destination for me. A city of a thousand images: sudden bay vistas and scudding white clouds; graceful suspension bridges and the brooding Alcatraz jail; steep hills and look-out posts; mist clinging to hillsides and high bridges; clanging, rattling cable cars and vintage trams; barking sea-lions and basking seals; chilly sea breezes and choppy ferry rides; Fisherman's Wharf and steaming clam chowder with crispy sourdough bread; hot chocolate from Ghirardelli's and the bustling shops of China Town. A sensuous city of whose sights, sounds, tastes and touch it was impossible to grow tired.

I had always considered the flight from London to San Francisco to be one of the world's great air journeys. It meant breakfast in England, lunch over Iceland, afternoon tea over Canada and supper in California, and the crisp clear northern air could usually be relied on to serve up a visual treat of a geography lesson. Iceland's snow dusted central plateau gave way to long northern fjords, serrated fingers of dark granite jutting out into bright blue seas with isolated red-roofed dwellings nestling beside sheltered inlets. Greenland's smooth white wilderness of broad sweeping snowfields and vast icy plateau, so pristine and so close in the crystal clear atmosphere, gave way to icy mountains, grey cliffs, tumbling glaciers and shattered ice-flows on its western shores.

Between Greenland and Baffin Island, the Davis Strait's seascape of broken ice flows and scattered icebergs led to vast ice fields, fringed by jagged fissures which merged and divided to form a mazy network of canals snaking across frozen Arctic seas. Baffin Island presented a sparkling white winter wonderland of angular peaks, snow filled valleys and sweeping glaciers. Hudson Bay passed as a mist shrouded grey mass. Through thin cloud, northern Canada offered an endless grey and white featureless tundra wasteland, frozen lakes gradually giving way to unfrozen, and tundra yielding to prairie. The high mountains of Washington and Oregon – Mount Whitney and Mount Rainier – marked our arrival in US airspace, and the distinctive lines of the San Andreas fault gave warning of imminent arrival in San Francisco. Within minutes, the blue Pacific was below, the white clouds clinging to the coastal hills enveloped us, and the waters of San Francisco Bay rose slowly to meet us.

Twelve years earlier I had been on board a flight from London which was twice struck by lightening on the approach to San Francisco airport, the jarring bolts entering through one wing and emerging through the other, but on this occasion we were spared such a dramatic welcome. In fact we didn't receive any welcome at all. According to the stamps in my passport, this was my fiftieth visit to the USA, and it seemed quite reasonable to expect that the authorities might mark the occasion by mustering a suitable reception party – the Vice President, the band of the US Marines or the Mayor of San Francisco, perhaps. But there was no one there to meet us, not even so much as a Deputy Commissioner for Public Sanitation.

Even the Department of Agriculture's friendly little spaniels, which usually poked around arriving passengers sniffing out contraband apples and oranges which might be harbouring ferocious foreign fruit flies or blight, had disappeared. Either they had been retired or had gone for a comfort break. The recollection of these busy little dogs was a reminder of a gentler era when the notion of a threat to national security was nothing more serious than an illicit banana or a smuggled satsuma. But the luxurious all-enveloping warmth which greeted us as we stepped from the terminal building onto the sidewalk immediately restored our spirits and our offended pride as we headed for the rental car offices.

I was prepared to excuse California's Governor Arnold Schwarzenegger for not being there personally to welcome us. He was probably tied up in a meeting in Sacramento, wrestling to solve the State budget deficit. I had in fact emailed Arnold to tip him off about the impending invasion of his State by a small task force of desperate Brits bent on a charitable mission, but he obviously hadn't got round to processing this alarming news. So we met no resistance as we broke out of the terminal building, penetrated the perimeter of the airport and staked out the Avis parking lot. I suppose he had a reasonable excuse for his lack of preparedness. The advantage of surprise was on our side, as I had only given him twenty four hours advance warning of our arrival. It seemed a prudent precaution to take. After all, he's bigger than me! Tangling with the Terminator was not to be undertaken lightly.

Arnold did eventually reply to my email, but not with any message of support from the Governor's Office or a charitable contribution to the project funds. He assured me that he was committed to restoring my confidence in state government and that with my help California would once again be the "Golden Dream by the Sea". I found it difficult to see how this could be a relevant response to my message, but perhaps comprehension of written English wasn't part of the Governor's job description.

We commandeered a rental car, a nondescript sub-compact product of present day Detroit, and plunged into the surging flow of the early rush-hour traffic. Skirting the western shore-line of the white-capped San Francisco bay, we headed north towards the Golden Gate Bridge. As we were due in Sacramento by the early evening, it was important that we resist the subtle blandishments of San Francisco and press on towards California's state capital.

It goes without saying that we totally failed to resist – it would of course be outrageous to be so close to San Francisco and not to turn aside. We headed down to the bustling Fisherman's Wharf area. Despite the fact that the airline had been repeatedly force-feeding us for the last twelve hours, we couldn't pass up the chance of a sustaining snack of clam chowder and sourdough bread. We took a stroll on breezy Pier 39, tram-spotted a few historic tramcars, checked that Alcatraz hadn't absconded and purchased a six months supply of Ghirardelli's famous drinking chocolate.

So it was not until much later that evening that we reached Sacramento, the home of our hosts for the night, and had our first glimpse of the vehicle that had drawn us from afar and would be our companion for the next few weeks, the stately and venerable Pontiac Grande Ville.

It was not exactly love at first sight! Like a huge blue and white beached whale lying on a concrete slab, the Pontiac looked decidedly vulnerable and fragile. Andrew's friend

Ben, a dapper dentist who was our host for the night and who had tracked down and purchased the vehicle for him, made the introductions. Ben could hardly be accused of being effusive in his praise. "It's one helluva long car. Takes a lot of getting used to the handling, and drives like a cloud – understeers badly. She's the mother of all gas guzzlers, you'll be lucky to get twelve miles to the gallon." (Actually, we struggled to get eleven miles to the gallon, but American gallons are a little smaller than British ones.)

He pointed out other downsides. "It takes a special trick to get the engine to fire. And the windows are loose." He wasn't kidding. The glass jangled alarmingly as the doors were slammed. When the driver's door was closed, a two inch gap opened up between the forward and rear side windows. It would definitely ship a lot of water in a storm. And there was more. Ben advised us to keep the air shocks pumped up (the what?). We should be sure to use the two metre wooden prop to support the hood - that's the 'bonnet' in English - if we wished to avoid instant decapitation in the desert.

Ben had been told that the soft top would fold down satisfactorily, although he hadn't tried it. It was fine - we tentatively flicked the lever and the top folded back slowly under the power of its own electric motor. And there were other positives too. The car had recently been serviced, and a new battery and set of tyres fitted. Ben believed that at some stage in its career - the car was over thirty years old - it had had a new engine installed. The sixty-four thousand dollar question was: would it make it to Chicago and back, a round trip of almost six thousand miles?

It was a big question, and there was no certain answer. We turned in for the night in a somewhat subdued frame of mind.

Chapter 2

The next day would be the first real test of whether we were likely to survive and how the Pontiac would shape up. To our delight – and surprise – it all went extremely well. The old girl – no, that's no way to refer to a thirty year old lady – floated majestically along the freeway, cutting a straight line through the heavy traffic with the nonchalant aplomb of an ocean liner slicing through heaving seas. The huge seven and a half litre motor purred comfortably as it lapped up the miles, and we reclined comfortably in the driving seats as if lounging on a pair of vast white leather sofas on wheels.

Down Interstate Ninety Nine, the north-south freeway which runs up California's central valley, the Pontiac jostled with juggernauts, raced with RVs, fought with four-by-fours and tangled with trucks. And all the time we made stately progress southwards at a steady fifty miles per hour. I was anxious not to fall foul of the California Highway Patrol, as I had reason to believe that my personal particulars were probably stored on their database of offenders, eagerly awaiting the opportunity to implement their 'three strikes and you're out' policy. I had once committed a minor traffic infringement by parking outside the stage door of a downtown theatre in San José. And ten years ago, on a busy highway in the Santa Clara Valley, I had been pulled over by a patrol officer on a motorbike and accused of the dreadful crime of driving a single occupancy vehicle in a carpool lane, an offense unknown in England. My gibbering pleas for mercy had clearly struck a chord with the officer, probably a sensitive family man beneath all that black leather. His sternly delivered admonition has stood me in good stead down the years. "In future, when in a foreign country, obey the laws of the land."

Throughout the day, the fabled cities of central California rolled past; Merced, Modesto, Fresno, Tulare, Marrakech, Samarkand (okay, cut the last two!) We gained sufficient confidence in our new vehicle to allow ourselves the luxury of a short detour off the freeway into the city of Merced to shop at a textiles store. Far away to our left, the distant snowcapped Sierra Nevada fringed the eastern horizon. Around us, stretching across the flat sun-baked landscape of the wide central valley of California, spread acres of grape vines and endless groves of citrus fruit. Herds of sad cows clustered apathetically on the brown earth of grassless cattle ranches. Warehouses and distribution depots, tractor franchises and railroad tracks, bordered the freeway. Concrete-lined irrigation canals drew straight lines across the landscape, heading for the San Joaquin River unseen over the horizon to our right.

By the time we reached Bakersfield in the late afternoon, the landscape had become more and more arid. In my view, Bakersfield would almost certainly have won any competition for America's least attractive town, the predominant architecture seeming to be grey rectangular blocks festooned with carbuncular growths of air conditioning plant, and the prevailing climate resembling that of a baker's oven. It was easy to resist making a stop. The previous year we had been driving in California and had, on the spur of the moment, made a quick diversion off the freeway into Bakersfield. The idea had been to buy some yoghurts at a store and to be back on the freeway within ten minutes. We never did find a grocery store and it took us almost an hour and a half to get ourselves back on the freeway. Bakersfield seemed very reluctant to yield up its prey. Visiting the place is a mistake people seldom make twice.

Beyond Bakersfield, the landscape took a decided turn for the better. As the highway rose towards the eastern foothills of the Sierra Nevada, the countryside became green, the groves of fruit trees reappeared and fir trees speckled the high hillsides. This higher ground was obviously more temperate and benefited from an appreciable amount of rainfall. As the road wound ever upwards through the long Tehachapi Pass, the scenery had a definite Scottish look to it. Away to the right and far below the road, we caught occasional glimpses of long freight trains grinding cautiously down the grade of the Tehachapi Loop. This remarkable feat of railway engineering, comprising a three hundred and sixty degree loop partly tunneled through the mountain, was constructed late in the nineteenth century. The locomotives of a freight train, often more than a mile long, would pass over (or under, depending upon direction) the final cars of its own train, the railroad equivalent of looping the loop.

At the head of the Tehachapi Pass, at an elevation of four thousand feet, lay the scattered township of Tehachapi. The greeting of the roadside signboard read, 'Welcome to Tehachapi - World Wind Energy Leader.' And they weren't kidding either. The hills were literally alive with the sight and the sound of windmills. Hundreds and hundreds of white propellers, crowding the steep green slopes and high hillsides and flecking the surrounding mountain ridges. A few were jumbo sized, most were mid sized, some had two blades, some had three. The scene had a hypnotic beauty. Everywhere propellers were turning, mesmerically drawing the eye away from the road and into the silver disc of perpetual motion. The eye involuntarily ranged from disc to disc, from group to group, hillside to hillside, ridge to ridge, counting numbers, spotting differences, discovering the occasional idle mill.

The 'World Wind Energy Leader' claim was no empty boast. Records show that the Tehachapi Wind Resource area is the largest wind energy producer in the world, producing as much wind energy as is produced elsewhere in the rest of the United States combined. And it produces more wind energy than Germany or Denmark or Japan, other regions with a high interest in the production of electricity from wind energy. I was happy to take on trust the statistic that there were more than 4,600 wind turbines in the Tehachapi area. These turbines collectively generated 1.4 billion kilowatt-hours of electricity per year, which – so we were reliably informed – could power nearly two million neon lighting fixtures. When the wind was blowing – and there was wind aplenty up here on the high ridges which separated California's central valley from the high desert - they collectively constituted a giant power plant which fed into America's electricity grid. Tehachapi power claimed to be the cleanest in the world, eliminating the environmental depredations linked with conventional fuels, which included destructive strip mining, coal fumes, atomic waste, and air pollution. As we drove through Tehachapi, were we looking at the rural landscape of the future, a model to be repeated the world over, wherever the wind blew? Possibly we were.

But right now, unless I could manage to keep my eyes on the road, it presented a real and present road safety hazard.

From the crest of the Tehachapi Pass, the landscape widened out as we drifted down the gentle grade towards the small and isolated desert community of Mojave, billed extravagantly as 'California's Golden Crossroads', the gateway to the Mojave Desert. Mojave was a cross roads town, with a couple of strips of motels and fast food outlets and precious little else. So it was somewhat of a surprise to catch sight of Mojave Airport slightly above the town. Ranks upon shiny ranks of airliners lined the tarmac and nosed onto the runways. It seemed to have more planes than London's Heathrow Airport. Was some major event taking place in the desert? A Presidential or Papal visit, perhaps? Where were all these planes going to? The answer of course was, nowhere. This was a vast dumping ground, or holding area, a car park for planes which were without work or looking for new owners. The hot dry desert climate provided the perfect conditions for storing planes safe from the deteriorating effects of wet and cold.

Having been confined to car seats for many hours, we gently eased ourselves from the vehicle outside our motel. We were instantly grasped by the rough desert wind and propelled towards the motel office. And after checking in, the same wind marched us firmly across the side street into a near-by restaurant.

Later that evening, the wind had dropped and we emerged from the restaurant into the rapidly deepening desert night. The vivid turquoise sky which silhouetted the surrounding mountains was creeping upwards, chasing and extinguishing the final fading embers of daylight. Within moments, the turquoise gave way to the soft velvet blackness of the desert night sky, and over our heads a canopy of ten thousand silent stars, unblinking, seemed almost within touching distance. Apart from the low rumble of a freight train moving slowly along the tracks beside the main road, the world seemed at peace. Life was looking good. We – and our Pontiac – had come successfully through the test of that all important first day.

America is extremely well endowed with vast numbers of motels, ranging from top brand luxury motels with heated indoor pools, hot-tubs and fluffy towels, through to cheap national chains and locally owned 'Mom and Pop' motels where standards of quality vary enormously. Because we would be travelling in a very distinctive vehicle, we reasoned that we owed it to her to be equally discerning in our choice of lodgings. We had decided therefore that on this trip we would treat ourselves to middle of the range branded motels rather than go for cheap and cheerful budget brands. The wisdom of this extravagant policy decision was apparent from the moderately extensive breakfast buffet, with three choices of cereal and two flavours of yoghurt, provided on this first overnight stop. Even the large cockroach which trekked slowly across the breakfast room floor was a better class of cockroach.

I returned from the motel office after settling the account to find Lois standing beside the Pontiac engrossed in earnest conversation with an elderly gentleman. He looked like an escapee from a hospital ward, carrying a surgical bag of fluid connected to intravenous drip tubes that disappeared into his pyjama leg. He was initially interested in our vast and splendid motorcar, which was apparently a very rare model, and quizzed us about the finer details of engine size and performance. Needless to say, we were totally ignorant of such matters. Could he buy the car from us when we no longer needed it? No offer price was discussed, but I promised to pass his particulars to the vehicle's owner.

At this point Vince, our new acquaintance, noticed the medical charity tee-shirts we were wearing, and we had our first introduction to what was to become a conversational routine with folks we met. It went like this. First, we would tell them why we were driving along Route 66 in such a dodgy vehicle, and explain that the disease for which we were raising funds was known in America as ALS, or Amyotrophic Lateral Sclerosis. It was more familiarly known as Lou Gehrig's Disease, after a baseball star who died in 1941. They would then tell us of an acquaintance who has or had the disease. And finally they would launch into their own life stories together with details of their medical histories and problems, and sometimes those of close relatives as well. The routine seldom differed. Perhaps they assumed we were doctors, perhaps we just had sympathetic faces, or maybe it had something to do with the breakdown of inhibitions out in the deserts and on the open road.

Vince was a semi-retired real-estate agent and he was keen to tell us about his own charitable interests. He was an enthusiastic proponent of the wonderful work done by a pioneering anti-cancer clinic in Los Angeles, and a keen supporter of an international fellowship which promoted interfaith reconciliation. His home town was Tehachapi, where he lived in his long silver RV motor home, now temporarily parked beside the motel in Mojave. Vince's present predicament had begun on a recent trip to Nevada. His foot had become septic and swollen up alarmingly, so he had checked into an accident and emergency clinic in the desert town of Mojave. The doctors had warned him that the infection had become so severe that he was in danger of losing his foot. His emphatic response had been that he had faith that his foot could be saved and that no way would he let them amputate it. The outcome was that he had been rigged up for intravenous antibiotic treatment, given a supply of dressings, equipment and medicines together with careful instructions in self nursing, and checked into a nearby motel. Happily for Vince, the foot seemed to be responding to treatment and prayer.

He was keen to tell us his story. A few years before, he told us, he had been going through an unhappy divorce experience when, he said, "The Lord met me. He gave me this wonderful book, a book to live by." He retreated with obvious discomfort to his room, and returned with a large Bible. So far, he told us, he had memorised 128 chapters of the Bible, including 110 of the Psalms of David. (I'm not sure if the 110 were additional to the 128 or included in the 128. In either case, it was a remarkable achievement.) He showed us a sheet of paper on which he had set out his reading programme, carefully scribed in tiny writing, detailing what he had read and when. He enthused about First Corinthians Thirteen and told us he was currently well into memorising the Book of Hebrews. As we parted, he told us he would be praying for us on our journey and asked us to pray for him.

(Weeks later, back at home in England, I received a letter from Vince. True to his word, he said he had been praying for us. "Late at night, into the wee hours of the morning, I am busy doing the work of the mighty Lord," he wrote. Sadly, Vince died eight months after our meeting at Mojave, and we were saddened by the death of a friend, albeit a friend we only met for half an hour.)

Under a clear bright blue morning sky, we bowled along the highway across the shimmering Mojave Desert, a vast flat expanse of sand and stones, speckled with stunted shrubs and occasional Joshua trees. Jagged mountains ringed the distant perimeter of the desert. Deep into the desert, we rolled past the saloons and old-style stores which lined the undulating main street of Barstow, a pioneer frontier town which oozed the spirit of the old wild west, despite the inevitable modern strip of car franchises, motels and fast-food outlets. We made the obligatory visit to the Barstow 'Route 66 Museum' to learn more about the route we were to follow, and did a spot of train spotting at the historic Mexican-style railroad depot, the Casa del Desierto or House of the Desert.

In fact, the town of Barstow owed its existence to the railroad and was named after the Santa Fé's president, William Barstow Strong. The settlement didn't exist until 1886 when the California Southern, a subsidiary of the Santa Fé Railway Co., completed its line from San Diego to join the Southern Pacific's transcontinental line which had opened three years earlier. The junction was at first known as Waterman, but changed its name to Barstow as a boot licking gesture to its greatest benefactor and main employer. Or perhaps the town fathers just thought that mellifluous Barstow was a prettier name.

Barstow developed as a kind of desert Doncaster, or a Californian Crewe, serving the transport needs of the rip-roaring silver and borax mining communities in the Calico Mountains just to the north of town. The silver mining business crashed when the price of silver collapsed, leaving nearby Calico as a ghost town populated by wild asses, but the town of Barstow had by then become established.

I once had an American colleague, raised in California, who spent his early years under the misapprehension that the name of the town was Bar Stool. It's not a bad name for a thirsty place in the middle of a parched desert. Before leaving town, we stopped by at the WalMart store to buy provisions, to check out the price of Hershey kisses, and generally to keep in touch with the everyday life of people who live in the desert. Inevitably, two guys in the parking lot wanted to know if our Pontiac was for sale. It was beginning to look like we were going to have to fight off potential buyers all the way to Chicago. How long would it be before we received an offer we couldn't refuse?

Chapter 3

Whilst arriving in Barstow was easy, leaving proved almost impossible. The lyrics of the popular hit song 'Hotel California' by the Eagles conclude with the lines, "You can check out any time you like, but you can never leave!", and the cities of California seemed to have enthusiastically adopted the same policy. We discovered that the general rule of American towns, and Californian ones in particular, was that they liked to keep their visitors, like flies in a spider's web, and that helpful signage to freeways or neighbouring towns must be strictly rationed. Barstow today, Merced yesterday, Bakersfield last year. Perhaps generations of insularity bred inhabitants who couldn't envisage that anyone might actually want to leave their towns. But after trying every available exit, and retracing our steps several times, we eventually found our way onto the old Route 66 heading east.

This was the old Route 66 of the postcards. Black top, two lane highway, the 66 shield stencilled neatly on the road surface every few miles, the desert rolling away on both sides. The car top folded back, the wind in the hair and the sun beating down. We passed the historic isolated Bagdad

Café, congratulating ourselves on the splendid progress we were making along the smooth, gently undulating highway. This was the film location of the 1988 comedy movie and subsequent TV series 'Bagdad Café', in which German tourist, Jasmine, abandoned by her husband in the Mojave desert made a new life for herself among the comings and goings of this rundown truck stop. Ironically, the Bagdad Café isn't at Bagdad – that's an abandoned town twenty miles further up the road. And it isn't really the Bagdad Café - its real name is the Sidewinder Café, but it subsequently metamorphosed into the identity of its film alter ego.

We were on a roll, and weren't even tempted to stop for a buffalo burger. Apart from the very occasional car travelling in the opposite direction, the road seemed otherwise totally deserted. But our complacency was punctured when the road surface abruptly deteriorated into a shattered, corrugated pavement, slowing us down to a painfully slow, bone shaking twenty miles per hour. To banish the spectre of our precious borrowed car dropping to pieces beneath us, we slipped onto the nearby freeway for a couple of junctions until the historic route had had time to mend its ways.

Well out of sight of the rushing freeway, the old road now passed through landscape akin to the surface of the moon. Arid shingle, lumpy black volcanic rocks and lava beds, the conical black protuberance of the extinct cinder crater of Amboy, dry lakes and creeks long devoid of water. For intrepid travellers of yesteryear, impoverished migrants displaced from their homes in the Midwest and the Great Plains and travelling westward in dilapidated vehicles, this could be a terrible place. Devoid of shelter from the searing sun, remote from human settlement and totally lacking in water sources, a breakdown here could literally mean the difference between life and death. Daytime temperatures here reach a hundred and twenty degrees Fahrenheit, conditions guaranteed to cruelly expose any weaknesses in the motor cooling system and precipitate mechanical calamity.

With distant grey mountains standing sentinel on every horizon, a gradually approaching noose of jagged peaks closed in on us, ahead and to right and left. To the right, the Bullion Mountains separated the hostile Mojave Desert from the benign Palm Springs resort region. To the left, the Bristol Mountains, the Cady Mountains and the Clipper Mountains successively barred the way to charred oblivion in the fiery furnace of a high rugged wilderness. Compensating for the almost total lack of fellow travellers on our route was the reassuring presence of a regular stream of growling freight trains on the transcontinental railroad which accompanied our road a discrete quarter of a mile or so distant. These inevitably comprised a posse of four, five, or six diesel locomotives labouring up the grade with a train of container wagons a mile long.

Now here's a remarkable phenomenon. For almost a thousand miles, across parts of California, Arizona and New Mexico, we travelled within sight of the railroad, making steady progress at around fifty miles per hour on our west to east journey. We saw dozens of these freight trains, but every single one was travelling in an east to west direction. So here's the big question. What do they do when they reach California? Are they all piling up in some vast marshalling yard? Do they scrap them, ship them across the Pacific to Asia, route them back east via Canada or Mexico, or send them back at dead of night? Answers should be submitted on a postcard, please.

But now our route pierced the girdling ring of mountains, merged with the freeway and drifted down from the elevated Mojave Desert into the community of Needles, a hundred and fifty miles from Barstow and the last town in California. Needles was the sort of place for which the description "middle of no-where" was coined. Surrounded by serrated rocky peaks, it lay at the backside of the Mojave Desert a dozen miles from California's border with Arizona, backing onto the equally inhospitable deserts of Arizona beyond the Colorado River.

It was somewhat of a relief to arrive safely in Needles. An enforced overnight desert stop among the scorpions and icy blackness of a Mojave night was not a prospect to be relished. Owing to bad experiences in the past, I possessed a morbid suspicion of the accuracy of fuel gauges, and for the final fifty miles of the hostile desert I had been anxiously eying the rapidly plummeting needle as the miles rolled by at a strictly non-'politically correct' rate of eleven miles per gallon. Our contribution to climate change was not something that occupied us at the time, but when fossil fuels have finally run out and when global warming has become irreversible fact of life, our roles as minor villains in the piece will probably merit at least a footnote in the history books.

We rolled into the first gasoline station in Needles. The chief mechanic strolled over and admired our vehicle. "Hey, you guys look like you're having way too much fun!" We tanked up with fuel, and our mechanic friend came over again. "Do you have air shocks? It looks to me like your rear suspension has gone. Mind if I put it up on the ramp for a moment?" Now I have a healthy suspicion of folks who tout for business from the weak and vulnerable. It wasn't at all clear whether we were dealing with a conman who wanted to relieve us of some dollars, or with a guardian angel who would help us to our destination. But, in truth, we had noticed that the Pontiac was low at the rear and that, from our position behind the steering wheel, the long blue hood appeared as an upward incline. So with nothing to lose, we watched nervously as our vehicle rose slowly towards the rafters.

The old vehicle meekly submitted to the indignity of some vigorous prodding and probing of the nether regions, which duly confirmed the worst. The suspension coils, clearly the thirty year old originals, were totally ineffective and the car was riding on its back axle. Given the load we were carrying and the rough terrain we were crossing, there was a big risk of the axle collapsing. The only thing that had been keeping us on an even keel had been the air in the air shock absorbers, and this had leaked away some time back.

At this point Hal, our friendly chief mechanic, played his trump card. "It might surprise you, but I've got a set of suspension coils for this car in my store room. I can have them fitted in fifteen minutes if you want." Hal was a big bear of a man and he had been fixing cars in the desert since 1962. How amazing that, in the middle of the desert, this guy had the parts for our thirty year old vehicle! Back in England, it could have taken days to get correct replacement parts from the local distributor – part of the ritual involves sending the wrong parts the first time round – assuming optimistically that they were still available for an older vehicle.

Twenty minutes later, we were off on the road again, although poorer by $240. But Hal had obviously been a guardian angel, and Vince had clearly been busy interceding! The Pontiac rode much better thanks to its new suspension. Ben had told us when he handed over the car that it "drives like a cloud". By this he had meant that the steering was vague and that the car floated and wandered, as in Wordsworth's lines, "I wandered lonely as a cloud". But now it sat up straight and steered crisply and responsively.

Leaving Needles, we headed for the Arizona border, from where we were due to make a fifteen mile deviation southwards to the resort of Lake Havasu City. This was not a deviation we were making by choice. On the freeway into Needles, and in the town itself, we had noticed groups of leather-clad bikers headed in the same direction as us. It was a Friday afternoon, and Needles and the neighbouring community of Laughlin were playing host to a bikers' convention. Hundreds of hairy bikers on Harleys and Hondas were noisily converging on the area from every direction. Every motel and lodging place for miles around was fully booked and we had been fortunate to book one of the last few rooms available, out at Lake Havasu City in the upmarket Ramada Hotel.

Within a few minutes of leaving Hal's ministrations, we had a new problem. The car engine had always had a slight whine, but it was nothing obtrusive and nothing which suggested any problem. But now it rapidly increased to become a penetrating screech, like a high pitched jet engine whine. We crossed the shining Colorado River and turned south towards Lake Havasu City, climbing up through a high desert pass lined by strangely shaped rocky outcrops, like twisted spires and pinnacles in a gigantic sculpture park, and steamed down the other side towards the distant urban smudge of the lakeside resort lying beside the glinting silver lake on the Colorado River.

Our noisy progress, screeching like a demented banshee, was no doubt driving every desert coyote and wild dog within a wide radius totally mad. It was having the same effect on us, too. Stress levels were running high and realisation was dawning that this journey was not going to be just a pleasant jolly, a carefree cruise as vehicle delivery drivers. This was some of the most isolated and harsh terrain in

America, and we were there as human guinea pigs, to tease out and to trouble shoot all the hidden faults which were surely lurking deep within the Pontiac's vast and venerable frame. And we had to deliver it to Chicago in good working order within ten days. It was a relief to be able to switch off the whining motor in the hotel car park.

The view from our hotel room window was impressive, featuring the wide expanse of the shining lake with the distant jagged mountain chain lining the horizon. Our experience with hotels around the world has taught us that it is usually a mistake to ask for a lake view room, as the computer system will then feel it is duty bound to allocate these awkward customers a room above the hotel kitchens with a view of the tradesmen's delivery bay and laundry room. No, the answer to this particular dilemma is to request a room overlooking the parking lot, with a partial view of the adjacent gas bottling plant. This inevitably confuses the computer system and usually results in the allocation of a splendid ocean or lake view room. The tactic seldom fails and at very least reduces the possibility of disappointment.

We put our mechanical worries to one side for a couple of hours, as we were keen to explore Lake Havasu City before the sun disappeared behind the mountain ridges. Lake Havasu is not a large lake – the local map shows it as a stomach shaped lake sitting below the alimentary tract of the Colorado River, of which it is a southward continuation. Lake Havasu City itself is a modern creation, incorporated as recently as 1978, and now home to over 46,000 souls. The story of the resort starts almost a decade earlier, when Robert McCulloch, an imaginative developer, made a winning bid of $2,460,000 to the British Government for the redundant 1920s-era London Bridge. This was taken down stone by stone, carefully labelled and shipped over from

England to Arizona. The rumour exists – and this may be an apocryphal story - that the developer failed to appreciate the deal's small print and thought he was buying Tower Bridge. Imagine the disappointment in unwrapping the package and finding that it was the wrong bridge!

Nevertheless, the bridge was reassembled in 1971 across a corner of Lake Havasu in Arizona's Mohave Desert (not the Mojave Desert, which is in California – how confusing is that for a name!), and the Lake Havasu City resort built around it. Surprisingly, the bridge fitted sympathetically into its new environment and looked remarkably natural. The promotional materials of the city authorities billed it as the "World's Largest Antique." What the custodians of the Great Pyramid at Cairo or the Coliseum at Rome make of this extravagant claim is not known.

Having escaped from the clutches of the bikers' jamboree, we discovered that Lake Havasu City was itself playing host to two major sporting events that week-end. There was the National Collegiate Triathlon Championships, and participants were much in evidence. Athletic young men and nubile young women in lycra shorts balanced precariously on narrow-tyred racing bicycles and paced the hotel walkways carrying spare wheels and helmets.

The second event being hosted was the Spring Heatwave Poker Run. We could see no visible manifestation of this exciting spectacle, and even had difficulty imagining what it might entail. It no doubt involved doing unspeakable things with fire-side implements! Or perhaps it was some sort of charity fun run for poker playing card schools, or was the American equivalent of welly-boot throwing or tossing the caber. Later research of the internet revealed the truth – this is powerboat racing, big business and a very expensive participant sport, conducted under the auspices of the American Poker Runs Association. One thing for sure – when Poker Running reaches the Olympic Games, the Americans will win gold, silver and bronze.

We wandered down to the Lake Havasu waterfront and explored the gift shops. Our British accents evoked concern and alarm among some of the locals. "Have you come to take the Bridge back?" one man asked us, but we graciously agreed to let them keep it. We were wearing our charity tee-shirts and the saleswoman in one shop was anxious to share her medical history with us. She related the story of how she was raised in the damp and hostile climate of the eastern seaboard, and had been a long term sufferer of chronic fatigue syndrome and fibromyelitis. Her doctors had wanted to put her in a wheelchair. She claimed that she had been supernaturally healed in her daughter's lounge while watching a Benny Hinn television programme. Hinn had announced, "There's a lady lying on a couch and the Lord's healing her!" Springing to her feet, she exclaimed, "That's me! I claim it in Jesus' name!" Apparently she had never looked back from that point, although she also acknowledged that the warm benign Arizonan climate had a significant part to play in her healing.

We paid for our postcards and made our exit, and headed for McDonalds to eat. While we were finishing our hot fudge sundaes, we spotted an elderly gentleman purposefully weaving his way through the tables to join us. He was wiry in build and serious in demeanour, and it came as no surprise that he wanted to tell us his story. He was, he told us, seventy six years old and four years ago had been diagnosed with Alzheimer's disease. Happily, his doctor had found a combination of drugs that suited him and was keeping the disease at bay, so he was still able to drive a car and fly a plane. (He didn't mention powerboats or whether he was also into poker running.) His father, he told us, had been a scholar and archaeologist, undertaking pioneering work in the Middle-East, and had written books about the development of religious thought. Sadly, his father had suffered a sudden stroke while on a holiday visit to Death Valley, and had slumped forward into his soup and passed away. Interesting things happen to our family, he said. For example, his Aunt Julia survived the London blitz, falling fourteen storeys in her bath tub when a bomb struck the building where she lived. We felt it was time to make our excuses and slip away.

We had exchanged names with our new friend and, on return home, I was able to check out the details of his story on the public internet. His father had indeed been an eminent churchman, archaeologist, and scholar of church history and Christian literature. A critical area of his scholarship had been tracking down and analysing the earliest known fragments of biblical texts and mapping these onto the traditional Byzantine text, the mediaeval body of documents which had been used as the source text for all the present day translations of the Bible, but which some alleged to have been cobbled together in the fourth century by an editorial board in Antioch. Partly as a result of this work, scholars had been able to conclude that today's Bible was both authentic and original. The essential details of his distressing demise were corroborated in the public record. Sadly, the internet was silent on the exploits of Aunt Julia.

But by now the purple fringes playing around the mountain ridges had long given way to a deep blue-velvet star-studded desert sky. It really was time to call it a day.

Chapter 4

Up bright and early next morning, with the early sun lighting up the mountains and bathing Lake Havasu in a gentle glow, we retraced our steps and re-crossed the Colorado River into California. Not many people know that although Arizona is technically in the Mountain Standard Time zone, it chooses to align itself with the time in California. We didn't know either, so we were a little confused about the real time when, engine whining impressively, we rolled on to Hal's forecourt in Needles. It didn't matter. Hal was there, and he didn't seem very surprised to see us back so soon.

The prime suspect for the noise was a loose fan-belt, but a quick inspection showed that there was nothing wrong there. Hal determined to give us a full mechanical healthcheck and promised to root out any deficiencies likely to jeopardise our smooth passage to Chicago. The catalogue of faults mounted: four loose nuts on the carburettor, a vacuum leak which was causing the ingress of unwanted air, a radiator fan which was wobbling on its bearings and likely to fly off into orbit at some future point, and a faulty alternator which was resulting in only a partial recharging of the battery.

After delivering his prognosis, Hal disappeared under the hood and set to work. A new alternator was ordered and miraculously arrived in a small van within twenty minutes, and a new fan-clutch was located in Hal's Aladdin's cave of spare parts. We had total confidence in the skills of our mechanical genie. Lois relaxed in the sunshine, reading a book and drinking Hal's complementary coffee, and keeping an eye on the comings and goings of hunky bikers. I took myself off on a self-guided walking tour of historic Needles – it only took a few minutes. Ninety minutes later, the car was starting sweetly and running smoothly and quietly, and we were back on the road again.

We crossed the swift ribbon of mercury that is the Colorado River for the third time, turned off the freeway onto the old Route 66 and headed north towards the town of Oatman. This was remote wilderness territory. We felt that, with our mechanical troubles now firmly behind us, we were now back in business again, and duly folded back the hood at the prospect of a hot day of al fresco motoring. We were looking forward to seeing Oatman, a former gold mining town deep in the Arizona desert but now a virtual ghost town. Ninety years ago it was home to about ten thousand souls, many of them miners and prospectors, but now only around a hundred and fifty folks live there. Oatman is reputed to be one of the hottest places on earth and it is possible to fry an egg on the sidewalk at midday. Occasional re-enactments of wild-west events are put on for tourists and the streets are roamed by wild burros, the descendents of asses turned loose when the mine closed down. Indeed, a veritable haven of isolation and tranquillity! At least, that's what the guide books would have us believe.

We were driving through dry, sandy, cactus speckled desert. The road rose gently through increasingly rock terrain. We started to meet the occasional trickle of bikers on the road, then streams, then torrents, all flowing towards Oatman. It seemed that Oatman was today's focus for the bikers' convention. We entered the town and crawled our way forward. Every available square inch of Oatman had been appropriated by bikers. Our car became a shiny blue and white island, conspicuous and motionless in a seething sea of black leather and chrome, tattoos, beards and beer-bellies. Ranks of gleaming Harleys were parked echelon style throughout the town, and the gentle burros had wisely taken to the hills. Groups of dismounted bikers thronged the highway, packed the raised boardwalk and stared at us sullenly from the doorways of old-west saloons and shops, like moody extras in a western movie. The spirit of censure was palpable. Through the car's open top we heard scathing muttered comments. "Fancy bringing a car like that through here today!" We felt like uninvited guests at a party, like unwelcome intruders at a private wake. Parking our vehicle was totally out of the question and we inched our way though and out of town.

Just outside the town, we passed the Gold Road goldmine which has been in operation, on and off, since 1900. Not much gold is mined there now, and the goldmine today is a tourist destination and serves as a venue for weddings. Couples have a choice of services provided by the mine staff. The complete wedding package consists of the ceremony, the preacher, reception and photographer, and the minimum package is just the ceremony and the preacher. The bride and groom are pronounced man and wife directly beneath Route 66 and, according to the promotional material, the only direction the marriage can go after that is up! The goldmine provides no facilities for the consummation of wedding nuptials, and recommends the honeymoon to be taken at the Oatman Hotel in town, a romantic eight bedroom lodging establishment built in 1902 whose claim to fame lies in the fact that Clark Gable and Carole Lombard spent their wedding night there in 1939.

Immediately after the goldmine, the road started to swing upwards. A series of hairpin bends followed, swinging left, then right, then left again as the narrow road soared steeply skyward. This was the notorious Sitgreaves Pass, which rose rapidly to an elevation of three and a half thousand feet. We had been blissfully unaware if its existence. Our map hadn't mentioned it and we had assumed that we would be travelling though flat desert terrain. This pass through the rugged Black Mountains had been the nemesis of many a pioneer traveller in the twenties and thirties, travelling in fragile over-laden vehicles with spindly wheels and tyres worn to the canvas. But the road had never been intended for vast vehicles such as our Pontiac, whose wheelbase covered almost the entire width of the road.

Reaching the summit of the Sitgreaves Pass, the amazing vista of the Arizona desert plateau suddenly opened beneath us, stretching northwards to the horizon and away into Nevada. Colourful rocky outcrops, spectacular canyons and mesas, a real life travel poster or a Marlborough advertisement. But there was no time to pause and admire the view, as the narrow road swung downwards through another series of tight hairpin bends, with scary unprotected precipices to the edges. Edging cautiously down the road, I was aware of a column of frustrated bikers following closely behind us. The leader of the pursuing pack was an aggressive individual in black leathers, and in the rear view mirror I could see him gesticulating vigorously. "Pull the effing thing over, can't you!" he stormed. I grudgingly complied when safe to do so. Any lingering feelings of charity which

I might have harboured towards him and his genre were severely strained.

We descended into Kingman, a quiet three-street town comprising a County Court, a County Jail and a few stores, surrounded by the usual periphery of gas stations, motels and fast food outlets. Close to the railroad tracks was the Route 66 Museum. This focussed very much on the human stories, the triumphs and tragedies of the thousands of migrants who travelled this route to the promised land of California, a fabled nirvana of sunshine and orange groves. Many were in search of riches, the good life and adventure. Others were reluctant travellers, escaping the grinding poverty, the all pervading red dusts and the inhuman evictions of the Oklahoma "dust bowl" era.

For these 'Okies', it was both a leap of faith and a journey of desperation. For them, the Highway 66 was a concrete ribbon of hope, girdling a continent from the Mississippi to the Pacific, threading the deserts and mountain passes and linking the Midwest and the Great Plains to a better life on sunny shores. For some, the leap of faith led to happy rewards, for many that faith was sorely tried in adversity. Sadly it was frequently a story of shattered dreams and dashed hopes. Apparently ninety percent of John Steinbeck's "Grapes of Wrath" generation of migrants in the twenties and thirties returned home within a few months, some being turned back by California state police at the California border, others made to feel unwelcome or unable to settle.

The 'Okies' were despised and resented by the local Californians, and the land and the jobs for which they had risked all were just not available. Thousands wound up in squalid squatter camps, hungry and harassed by police, at the mercy of flood, famine and disease, ignored by uncaring officialdom. They discovered that the farming lands of California were controlled by huge impersonal agribusinesses, and that the life of the casual seasonal harvest workers was one of exploitation and servitude. It was a case of the grass not being greener on the other side, and with the news of improving times back home, some took the Route 66 eastward like returning prodigals. Many others had failed to make California due to illness, accident and mechanical breakdown en-route. Rutted roads and rickety vehicles, leaking radiators and threadbare tyres, exacted a cruel toll under the unrelenting sun of the harsh desert and the freezing nights of the high plateaus. Some thwarted travellers settled at intermediate destinations close to where they came to a halt, others eventually found their way back east.

Following the trail of these returnees, we headed east out of Kingman. In contrast to the challenges of previous stages of the journey, the hundred and fifty mile section of historic Route 66 from Kingman to Williams was a piece of cake. Arcing through the Arizona plateau on a trajectory perhaps twenty miles north of the modern freeway, the two lane highway was smooth and virtually devoid of traffic. It was well maintained by the state of Arizona because it provided the only road access to a number of remote and scattered communities which had survived along the way. Frequently as straight as a die, a long section passed through the Hualapai Indian Reservation. Friendly skies soared above us, and the wide-open landscape stretched to the distant horizon. Occasional Route 66 curios, such as the idiosyncratic Hackberry General Store with its crumbing jalopy and antique gasoline pumps, sprinkled the route. Having created a minor traffic jam, an air ambulance rose from the tarmac a few hundred yards ahead, headed perhaps for a hospital in distant Flagstaff. On the railroad which paralleled the highway half a mile to the south, a steady stream of slowly moving freight trains growled their way westward.

Driving across this plateau from Kingman in the west to Flagstaff in the east involved a distance of a little over two hundred miles, and the overall impression was that the route was pretty well level. In practice, the Arizona plateau seemed to be on a tilt, as if some giant creature had stepped on its edge. It rose smoothly and almost imperceptibly from two and a half thousand feet in elevation at Kingman to around seven thousand feet at Flagstaff two hundred miles distant. Leaving Kingman, the terrain was treeless semi desert, cactus-free with just a little scrub among sand and gravel, but very soon giving way to scattered "pygmy" pines, squat green blobs of fir trees scattered thinly over the parched landscape. Moving upslope, the average temperature decreases and the overall precipitation increases.

The gradual change in the vegetation is distinctive as these "pygmy" pines, which are juniper trees, gradually grow taller, less squat and more pervasive, becoming at the western end of the plateau a well wooded landscape of stately pines. In the popular image, Arizona is desert country, but in practice almost a quarter of its surface is covered by these pinyon-pine and juniper woodlands which then merge into ponderosa pine forests further upslope. In fact Flagstaff, at seven thousand feet one of America's highest cities, lies at the centre of the world's largest ponderosa pine forest, the Coconino Forest.

Twenty miles or so before the town of Williams, we stopped in the little community of Seligman, once a busy Route 66 town but now sparsely populated and tending towards ghost town status. Seligman was a one street town, and a walk round the block towards the site of the former railroad station confirmed that most properties, including the historic dance hall and brothel, were now vacant lots. But what the current inhabitants lacked in numbers they made up in character. We called at the general store cum barber shop and talked to Angel Delgadillo, the sprightly septuagenarian barber and a Route 66 celebrity. Learning that we were from England, he enquired which side of fifty we were. Having established that we had indeed reached the big five-oh, he conspiratorially fished out a magazine from a secret cache of literature. It was a risqué back number of Britain's Saga magazine for 'Seniors' and he modestly showed us a feature article about himself! Angel had lived all his life in Seligman and had been trimming hair for most of that time. He was widely credited as the creator of, and the impetus behind, the National Route 66 Association and the road's rebirth as a nostalgia phenomenon. We caught up with him just before he was due to leave for his Saturday afternoon nap, and he graciously consented to be photographed sitting in his barber chair.

Across the street was the Snow Cap Café owned by his eccentric elder brother Juan where, like all his customers, we first had to run the gauntlet of Juan's zany sense of humour. "Sorry, we're open!" said the neon sign, and we fumbled awkwardly with the door handle, inconveniently fitted to the hinge side of the door. A small cup of coffee was served – in a thimble! A diet coke? – the straw proffered was straight out of the corn field. A napkin, sir? – a bunch of slightly used ones was offered, before a clean one. Cockroaches and artificial ketchup figured in the routine. The menu included 'Hamburger without Ham', 'Cheeseburger with Cheese', and 'Dead Chicken'. On the forecourt outside the restaurant stood Juan's bizarrely decorated old Chevrolet, a cut-down touring car decorated like an out of season Christmas tree and dripping with simulated icicles to reflect the 'Snow Cap' theme. Keeping a watchful eye on the proceedings was a stuffed owl, perched on the top of gas pumps which hadn't pumped gas for many years. On reflection, I'm convinced that Juan was a totally misunderstood man. He was clearly a marketing genius! No-one left town without partaking at his Snow Cap café!

Fortified by Juan's coffee, we returned to the Pontiac, which we had parked top folded back outside the barber shop, to find it being admired by an elderly motor enthusiast. "I've never seen one like this before!" was his verdict. He obviously knew a thing or two, as we later discovered that less than three thousand of this particular specification and vintage were ever made. The other two thousand nine hundred and ninety nine were probably broken up, corroded through or pensioned off long ago. Ours had been preserved by California's benign climate. I was slow to see a business opportunity and possibly missed a lucrative sale.

By the time we reached Williams, the sun had begun to decline and the temperature had dropped drastically, and we were happy to exchange the open top motorcar for a snug motel room.

Pontiac Grande Ville

The old desert road, near Barstow, California

Extinct cinder crater at Amboy, Mojave desert, California

London Bridge in the desert, Lake Havasu, Arizona

Holbrook, Arizona, and environs

Sleep in a Wigwam, Holbrook, Arizona

The Continental Divide, New Mexico

Established 1603 in Santa Fé, New Mexico

Chapter 5

Williams had the distinction of being the last town on the entire Route 66 to have been bypassed by the opening of the new freeway. It was a typical two street town but unlike many others on the old Route 66 it seemed to have survived and thrived. The town was proud if its Route 66 associations, and the historic business district and the buildings lining the main street have been designated a local heritage area. By the good fortune of its geography, Williams had been able to reinvent itself as the 'Gateway to the Grand Canyon', fifty miles to the north, and the starting point of the tourist train which delivers visitors directly to the south rim of the canyon.

For us, the closeness of the Canyon was a real temptation, a diversion and distraction which called for self denial and singleness of purpose. After all, we had an objective to achieve, a vehicle to deliver in good order, a route to follow and a deadline by which we must reach Chicago. So of course, we did the right thing – we yielded to temptation. Turning the nose of the Pontiac northwards, the bright early morning sunlight belying the fact that the outside temperature was but a whisker above freezing, we headed through the pines towards the Canyon.

The Grand Canyon is rightly regarded as one of earth's most amazing geographical phenomena. Many excellent books describe this mile deep, ten mile wide, fifty mile long gash in the Arizona plateau with its spectacular and ever changing colours, canyons and rock formations. This was not our first visit, but I don't think the Canyon will ever lose its ability to impress. Because the Grand Canyon is so remote from major population centres, the numbers visiting on any day are constrained by the amount of lodging available in the immediate neighbourhood and in the hinterland within travelling distance. It doesn't get swamped by vast hordes of casual day trippers. So we joined the modest number of early Sunday morning tourists taking in the vistas from one of the first viewpoints.

Peaceful reveries were shattered as the thin mountain air was suddenly rent by a penetrating and plaintive call. "That fence is there for a reason! For crying out loud Charlie, you'll kill yourself!" Every head spun in the direction of the despairing voice. It came from the direction of two young men, thirtyish, immaculately attired in Sunday best, camera toting, and obviously brothers. The younger one was patently bent on driving the elder to distraction, the elder was clearly of an attention seeking disposition and unperturbed by being the subject of public gaze. For a few minutes, peace reigned once more. Then the airwaves jangled. "What am I going to tell mother? That you died in the Grand Canyon? Why do you make me swear even on holiday? Even my boss says I swear too much!"

We wandered back to our car and moved on to the next viewpoint half a mile further along the canyon rim. A small change of viewpoint brought a fresh orientation and a new but equally splendid panorama. A different group of tourists lingered and gazed. An ear tingling wail assaulted the ears. "I don't belieeeeve it! You're headed out for that rock! Are you insane, Charlie?!"

We moved on, and the remainder of our Grand Canyon visit was idyllic. We took a sun-baked three hour hike along the rim trail, beyond the reach of the majority of car-bound visitors, out to Hopi Point with spectacular views westward and secret glimpses of the tiny Colorado River threading through the canyon a mile below. But we were now on borrowed time, and reluctantly turned back along the deserted rim trail towards the visitor centre where our Pontiac was parked. Peace and solitude reigned. Rounding a corner of the trail, the ether crackled. "For pity's sake, Charlie, let's try keeping to the trail for a change! What am I going to tell mother?!" We instinctively knew it really was time to hit the road again.

We left the Canyon area and lanced through the tall pines of the vast Coconino Forest in the direction of Flagstaff. The San Francisco Peaks dominate the approach to Flagstaff, visible from probably seventy miles in all directions, a snow-capped cluster of jagged summits which rises in splendid isolation from the Arizona plateau to the north of the town. We threaded the outskirts of Flagstaff and the historic downtown area without stopping, chose not to take the modern freeway out of town, and exited the city on the original Route 66 parallel to the railroad tracks.

Sounds easy, doesn't it? But this was our second experience (the first had been in Barstow) of a scenario that repeated itself many times over the next two thousand miles. The problem was this. Route 66 has been decommissioned as a national highway, so it doesn't appear on the road maps. On-route signage was irregular and inconsistent, provided by volunteers of the various state Route 66 Associations. The brown Route 66 shield appeared beside the route spasmodically. But at road junctions and intersections, when a split second decision had to be taken, there was nothing at all. We were travelling west to east, but all the Route 66 literature assumed travel from east to west!

Think about this example. 'After crossing the railroad, veer right and make a left at the second cross-road, follow the road to a T-junction where a right will bring you eventually into the town centre.' Now transpose these instructions for the reverse direction, add a couple of one-way streets for interest, and allow for the fact that 'after crossing the railroad' could mean a hundred yards after or five miles after. Not surprisingly, we frequently had to retrace our steps and depend on intuition, guess-work, prayer and solar navigation. (Even navigating by the sun wasn't an option at five o'clock on a rainy afternoon in the run-down back ways of suburban Carterville, Missouri.) Stress levels could shoot right off-scale. It would have been nice, but quite untruthful, to report that our debate was always calm and rational. But against all odds, and thanks to the accomplished and patient navigation skills of the co-driver, time and again we achieved remarkable miracles of precision route finding.

After Flagstaff, the trees and scrub gave way to vast grassy plains. Parched, dry grasslands stretched to the horizon and it took a very simple leap of imagination to visualise the time when buffalo roamed the range, shadowed by bands of Indian hunters, and pioneers crossed the landscape in narrow wheeled covered wagons. This terrain in turn gave way to empty inhospitable desert, red sand and shingle, red sandstone bluffs and isolated tufts of yellowing grass. Half a mile to the south, a procession of freight trains on the Santa Fé railroad toiled up the grade. Away in the distant north, were the shining colours of the Painted Desert, rocky outcrops, bluffs and cliffs.

At Holbrook, Arizona, the red sun was setting on the desert horizon as we checked into our lodgings at the Wigwam Motel and met our host Cliff Lewis. The notice outside read "Have you slept in a wigwam lately?" This was clearly a gap in our life experience which we ought to rectify. We had been keen to stay at the Wigwam Motel which is a well known Route 66 institution, where twenty or so concrete wigwams offer comfortable if basic accommodation. Adding to the historic ambiance, a 1950s or 1960s period car (non-runners, probably) was parked beside each wigwam, and our 1970s vehicle slotted in among these very sympathetically. Mr Cliff – my telephoned reservation had been taken by his brother Mr John – explained to us how the motel had been created by their father – Mr Chester – in 1950. "Everything is totally original," he told us. "We haven't changed even the furniture since our father built them."

We inspected our accommodation with interest. Thankfully the sheets and towels appeared to have been changed more recently (that day actually) and the television was modern. But the bedspread and the cane furniture were certainly 1950s. And the vast heating contraption was truly antediluvian. Mounted on the wall beside the front door, it comprised two vertical elements each about five feet high and four inches in diameter, mounted in parallel in front of an enormous reflecting device, all imprisoned behind a brown enamelled grill. At least, I assumed it was for heating – it may have been a patent mosquito exterminator. Thankfully we didn't need to use it.

We ate well at the Butterfield Stage grill just half a block along the street, an original 1929 eating establishment complete with authentic wooden sidewalk and frontage. Then, secure in our concrete wigwam, we slept well. In the middle of the night, I was jolted out of a deep sleep as the horn of the Pontiac, which was parked just a few feet from the wigwam's front door, began to sound furiously. Clearly this was an electrical fault – a short-circuit probably – and the next thing would be the motor springing to life. I froze under the bedclothes, expecting that at any moment the two ton vehicle would come bursting through the front door. Nothing happened, and realisation dawned that it was the claxon of a freight train passing on the Santa Fé Railroad a few yards away.

After a quick walking tour of Holbrook in the early morning, we concluded that we had chanced on the only town in the USA where it was impossible to buy breakfast. By eight thirty we were headed out into the desert on a lonely single track highway towards the south-east, red gravely sand with a few isolated tufts of dry grass stretching to the horizon in all directions. As the miles rolled by, the overwhelming impression was that we were the only living people left on earth. It was with some relief that we eventually turned northwards into the entrance to the Petrified Forest National Park. Our physical and mental equilibrium was restored by an intake of coffee and excellent hot cinnamon rolls in the refreshment corner of the National Park concession store.

The Petrified Forest National Park is linked to the contiguous Painted Desert National Park. My rudimentary understanding of the geography is that, aeons ago, the area had been forested. These forests had then been overtaken by swamp conditions which had preserved the fallen trees. An era of global warming had changed the area to desert, and wind erosion had eventually exposed the now petrified fallen trees. I think that was the gist of it, but the bottom line was that there were lots of fascinating stone trees to look at in the desert. For us the charm of the experience included the hot sun, open top motoring, spectacular desert vistas of vivid multihued rock and sand formations stretching away to the distant horizons in the north and west, and the selfishness of having the place almost to ourselves.

Midway through the Park, we spied an intriguing sign pointing away from the main highway, saying, 'To the Petroglyphs.' This was an irresistible attraction because, like every other curious person, it has always been our ambition to see petroglyphs! We parked in the small parking lot just as a coach-load of Japanese tourists arrived and followed these visitors along the narrow walkway towards an enclosed viewing area of desert overhang equipped with mounted telescopes. We were agog to see the petroglyphs, whatever they might be!

We discovered that petroglyphs are rock carvings created by the native people who lived in the area a thousand years ago. Carved into the flat rock faces of two huge boulders down on the desert floor, these examples of aboriginal art are extensive and explicit, and are reckoned to be the best examples of petroglyphs in the south-western USA. But the most remarkable feature was the fact that they were exceedingly rude! The charitable explanation was that they were probably linked with astrology and fertility rites. In today's society they would have either been banned as pornographic or displayed in the Tate Gallery.

We hit the route again and headed eastwards into New Mexico. The landscape of western New Mexico continued the pattern set by the Arizona high plateau prior to the interlude of the Painted Desert National Park, and although elevations of around seven thousand feet were noted, the greenery and heavy forestation which we met at the same elevation around Flagstaff was absent. I'm not a climatologist, but I assume from this that western New Mexico lies in a rain shadow which cuts off precipitation. Terrain of scrub and stunted fir trees gave way to desert areas where we passed close to dramatic red cliffs and rocky outcrops. This in due course gave way to prairie, miles of wide yellowish parched grasslands, and finally made a long and gradual descent from the high open prairie towards the city of Albuquerque.

Many miles of the route through eastern Arizona and through New Mexico (possibly most of the route, in fact) passed though Indian Reservation lands. This territory, which covers an area the size of the state of West Virginia, is the home of the Navajo Nation, and the presence of these Native American folk gave this section of the route its own distinctive character. We passed many settlements and villages, with clusters of one-storey homes, trailer homes, shacks and pick-up trucks. Poverty is a comparative thing, and there is no doubt that these people live in much poorer circumstances than most of their fellow Americans. Unfortunately, I don't know enough about the past wrongs or present injustices suffered, so it would be churlish of me to try to sound like an authority. But it seemed to me that these folks were in somewhat of a trap; living in their own reserves on land 'given' to them by the Federal government, they don't have access to the jobs of the developed US economy, and their land is arid and unworkable from an agricultural perspective.

Along the highway we passed many Indian trading posts – with unexciting names such as Indian City, Indian Ruins and Indian Market – and big billboards inciting us to turn off the route to buy Indian crafts and jewellery. But it appeared that 'paleface' travellers have become bored of Indian artefacts, that the romance and the lure of the Red Indian heritage has been dulled by familiarity and time. The parking lots at the trading posts looked empty. Maybe too the largesse of US government handouts has created a culture of dependence and complacency. After all, why go to Chicago (where it's bitterly cold in winter) and struggle for that poorly paid job, when you can stay on the reservation and enjoy year round sun. But I did notice a job opportunity for a smart entrepreneur. There must be a fortune to be made by someone who can work out how to harvest and recycle the multitude of scrap cars and the junk yards which litter the landscape in these parts.

We drifted down the long gradient from the high plateau and rolled into Albuquerque, tired and in need of lodgings. Stretched high across the roadways, banners were advertising the '22nd Annual Gathering of Nations Pow-Wow'. This, although we weren't aware of it at the time, is a jamboree which takes place every year in late April at the University of New Mexico's Arena in Albuquerque. It sounded like a big Eisteddfod with tomahawks. Thousands of Native Americans from across the USA and Canada, representing up to five hundred different tribes – Cheyenne, Seminole, Iroquois, Blackfoot, Mohawk, Choctaw, Chippewa, Cree, Lakota, and so on - converge on Albuquerque to celebrate Native American culture, music, dancing, food and crafts, and to crown Miss Indian World. This year the winner had been Miss Delana Smith, a member of the Ojibwe tribe from distant Minnesota and a primary school teacher. Her dancing skills, character and knowledge of tribal matters had enabled her to beat off strong competition from a field of rivals which included Miss Bazil-Lu Windy Boy, Miss Dawn Little Thunder and Miss Elizabeth Johnny John.

We became somewhat apprehensive. Having been squeezed out of Needles by squadrons of bikers on Harleys and Yamahas, we now faced the prospect of being frozen out of Albuquerque by bands of Indians in pick-up trucks and beat up Toyotas. Fortunately for us, the Pow-Wow had finished the day before our arrival and most of the participants had now left town. There was 'room at the inn' for us. In fact, there was also room for us in the inn's pool and jacuzzi – but only just. We shared them with an extended family of Navajos who were clearly big-time contributors to the profits of the American fast foods industry. The water level fell when they called it a day. Obesity in America – which is patently becoming a major national affliction – is no respecter of race, age or gender.

It was interesting to note the media debate which was ongoing. After all, I'm very interested in food. As a trained chef (not many people know that I have studied at URSC, Britain's University of Ready, Steady Cook!), food is one of my weaknesses, and if it's available, I can be tempted. The hub of the obesity debate is this; does the responsibility lie with the individual to exercise self control, or is it the responsibility of the food seller who has supplied and promoted the offending nutrients? One restaurant chain had billboards promoting a new menu item: "New! – Italian Chicken Melt". It comprised a long bun, chicken, cheese and French fries; how healthy is that, and would it be found in the trattorias of Tuscany? In America's litigious society, many of the fast foods vendors were getting anxious, and healthy menus and sensible portion sizes were beginning to put in an appearance. Several evenings – sometimes there was no other option in small communities – we ate healthily at McDonalds, choosing nutritious salads of grilled chicken. Even Kentucky Fried Chicken, the champion of all things fried, was urgently trying to reposition itself. This clearly posed a challenge for a company that has spent half a century reinforcing 'Fried' as an integral part of its brand image. The American public has now begun to link frying with dying, and may not yet be ready for KFC to reinvent itself as Kentucky Roasted Chicken. KFC lost an important round in the propaganda battle when adverts extolling the high-protein, low-carb character of its fried chicken (but relegating negatives about fat, cholesterol and sodium to the tiny print) were withdrawn on complaint. The latest KFC menu of baked chicken strips with rice, green beans and red peppers doesn't sound so 'finger lickin' good'!

Of course, the publicity surrounding the Atkins diet was influential in setting the vogue for carbs, or more accurately, for low-carbs, with carbohydrates becoming the latest dietary demon. Food stores and restaurant chains hyped their wares. We saw: Lo-Carb now by the Half Gallon (a half gallon of what?); Carb friendly Chicken Club Wraps; Lo-Carb Beer; even, Low-Carb Bread. USA Today ran a touching little news item reporting that many Americans on lower incomes can't afford to eat 'Low-Carb'. But am I missing something? Surely a low carb diet could mean one less burger bun, and make mine a small fries, please.

Chapter 6

Santa Fé, to the north of Albuquerque, lay on the earliest routing of the Route 66, although it was subsequently bypassed in the 1930s by a new direct east-west section of highway between Santa Rosa and Albuquerque. But as far as we were concerned, Santa Fé was a 'must see' element of our journey. A number of years ago a scheduled business trip to Santa Fé had, to our disappointment, been cancelled. It had been one of those business conventions where the content was so crushingly boring that the organisers, in order to attract delegates, had spiced up the event by selecting an exciting location and an interesting programme of side visits. The disappointment still rankled and this was an opportunity to put things right and discover what we had missed in Santa Fé.

Santa Fé is the town's lazy name; strictly speaking its full name is La Villa Real de la Santa Fé de San Francisco de Asis, which translates as the Royal City of the Holy Faith of St. Francis of Assisi. Not many people call it that nowadays. Lying at an elevation of seven thousand feet where the desert meets the Sangre de Cristo (Blood of Christ) mountains, the city was founded by the Spanish conquistadors in 1607 and as such it predates even the Plymouth settlement of the Pilgrim Fathers. The crisp mountain air, the clarity of the light and the warmth of the colours combined to make the place a magnet for generations of artists. More recently it became a favourite destination for backpackers, hippies and escapees from the rat race. But the lifestyle seekers have grown up or moved on, and the city has settled into a new phase of quiet and comfortable maturity.

Even today, it is has a distinctly European and Spanish air, with its laid-back atmosphere, adobe style architecture, St Francis' Cathedral and town plaza. The intimate downtown shopping streets are laid out in European proportions. The Palace of the Governors, an historic adobe building facing the green oasis of The Plaza, dates from the early seventeenth century and must be the oldest occupied building in the USA. Despite its greater antiquity, Santa Fé does not attract anything like the historical interest given by Americans to younger upstarts like Boston, Philadelphia and Williamsburg back east. I suppose the reason is that despite its history, it isn't perceived as being American history. Santa Fé was in fact the capital of a Mexican province until it was captured by the US army as recently as 1846. Santa Fé didn't disappoint us, but after a couple of hours exploration and a ritual fajita from a sidewalk vendor in the tree shaded plaza, the open road called us again and it was time to move on.

After some initial navigational frustrations, we rejoined the eastwards bound route and discovered that the eastern half of the state of New Mexico was quite different from the western half through which we had already passed. For one thing, it seemed to be almost devoid of significant settlements and human habitation. The Indian camps had all but disappeared. And who had ever heard of Santa Rosa and Tucumcari, the largest, in fact the only, two towns for a couple of hundred miles? We passed through a succession of small townships, now pathetically deserted, the houses, motels and gas stations derelict ruins, eloquent testimony to shifting economic fortunes. The prosperity that the old Route 66 had brought to the area – lodgings, eating places, gasoline stations, repair shops - had moved away with the building of the freeway. There was precious little else to sustain the population and they too had drifted away.

We stopped in Santa Rosa, an isolated town of three thousand people a hundred miles south-east of Santa Fé. Santa Rosa was a drab little town on a characterless tract of the New Mexico plateau, but it was obvious that there were some dedicated marketing people in the town hall. We learned that one of Santa Rosa's claims to fame was that it had been the location for a dramatic railroad sequence in the film version of 'The Grapes of Wrath'. I haven't seen the film, but I have read the book and am pretty sure that the story didn't include any railroad incident.

Despite the unfavourable odds handed out by geography, the town of Santa Rosa had managed to survive and was busy promoting itself as a water sports and scuba diving destination. This seemed a pretty unlikely role in such an arid and land-locked environment. On a scale of improbabilities, this came somewhere between mountain biking in Holland and camel racing in Ireland. But the civic marketing material told us that the town's crown jewel was its famous 'Blue Hole', a deep natural artesian spring which remained a constant sixty four degrees all year round.

We preferred however to keep our clothes on and opted to visit Bozo and Anna's Route 66 Classic Car Museum, where our 1974 Pontiac Grande Ville would have made an impressive addition to an already superb collection. We had assumed we were travelling incognito, but it seemed that the impending arrival of a couple of exiled Scousers was expected. As we entered the museum, the welcoming strains of Gerry and the Pacemakers' 'Ferry Across the Mersey' were issuing from the public sound system.

Our destination for the night was Tucumcari, a further seventy miles east across a vast treeless prairie of coarse grass and yucca, almost flat to the horizon on every side. We crossed occasional small rivers which actually contained thin trickles of water, unlike the dry river beds of the last five hundred miles. A succession of ghost settlements, long abandoned to decay, marked the route. Cuervo, which at its heyday had two hotels, two schools and two churches, now offered a derelict gas station, post office and Baptist church. In Newkirk, the cracked structure of the old church stood beside the highway. It must have been many years since the circuit riding preacher hitched his horse, but the cross still stood, slightly askew, high above the door of the wooden entrance porch. At Montoya, Richardson's Store and Gas Station stood crumbling behind a strong chain fence. A couple of abandoned cars stood sadly at the old pumps, as if patiently awaiting the day of rebirth, when gas might once again be pumped, and Oreos and Hershey Bars be purchased in the old country store.

But despite the discouraging evidence of decline along the route, we still felt pretty confident that we would find accommodation in Tucumcari, barring an unexpected kite flyers' or hot-air balloonists' convention. After all, it was the lodging capital of eastern New Mexico and regular roadside billboards had been proclaiming 'Tucumcari Tonite – 2000 Rooms' before we had even reached Albuquerque.

Threatening clouds were gathering and the light was fast beginning to fade as we reached Tucumcari, the last town in

New Mexico and close to the Texas border. In the motel car park, we lingered in the security of the Pontiac, reluctant to venture out into the inhospitable gathering gloom, as black sacks scudded across the bleak treeless landscape chased by an unrelenting wind. Not surprisingly, there was no convention being held in town and we successfully checked in, although the reception clerk had real difficulties handling such exotic visitors. England? How do you spell it? That's foreign isn't it? Even the computerized reservation system had problems coping with us, but it eventually registered us as guests from the US state of ENG.

The motel was beginning to fill up with other guests, weary car-borne refugees from the nearby freeway for whom the bright lights of Tucumcari represented a convenient mid-point stop-over in the long drive from, say, Dallas to Phoenix. We needed to brave the outside world again to eat. Pointing ourselves vaguely in the general direction of the nearby diner, our feet scarcely touched the ground as we allowed the wind to carry us across fifty yards of grass and in through the front door.

The restaurant was having a very busy evening – dining being one of the few available leisure activities in Tucumcari on a cold and blustery Tuesday night – and we engaged in a spot of people-watching as we waited for our nachos to arrive. Most of the clientele were clearly travellers, flotsam and jetsam from the tide of traffic swept along the Interstate 40, diners who were wishing they were anywhere but Tucumcari. There were just a few locals eating. This being Bible belt and Tuesday, the rest of the locals were probably at prayer meetings. The middle aged lady manager, severe and unsmiling, was a human pocket dynamo as she raced between tables, kitted out in close-fitting jogging pants tucked into white socks. Tucumcari might be the lodging capital of the entire Mid-West – and tonight Tucumcari was doing what it was good at, caring for the strangers in its midst - but Fifth Avenue's position as the fashion capital of the USA was safe.

I decided to check out Tucumcari's ambitious claim to have two thousand lodging rooms. Was this twenty motels of a hundred rooms, or forty motels of fifty rooms, perhaps? An analysis of the local yellow pages phone book in our room threw up some interesting statistics about the town. There were twenty seven motels, twenty gasoline stations and seventeen churches. Presumably Tucumcari also had some local inhabitants, although we had noticed no signs of housing, local shops or public buildings. Where do they hide the five thousand people who, according to the town's website, live here? The only evidence that we could see of an indigenous population was the vast car wrecker's yard, carpeting a considerable acreage beside the highway with rusting hulks.

It's an interesting thought that two thousand years from now, when all other vestiges of our present civilization have vanished, a future generation of archaeologists will be sifting through vehicle fragments in the desert and constructing hypotheses about social and economic structures in the 21st century. The debates in the learned journals will be about the societal implications of the discovery of the bones of a hitherto unknown variant of Buick, and the unexplained preponderance of Hondas and Hyundais over Chryslers and Chevrolets deposited in the late 20th century strata.

I had no intention that our splendid vehicle should end up in such an automobile graveyard, either in Tucumcari or anywhere else. I know very little about what goes on under the surface of a car, but what I did know was that we – two mechanical ignoramuses – had jetted into America, picked up an old car of unknown provenance and uncertain order, and immediately set off across hundreds of miles of desert and mountains, some of the most inhospitable terrain in the hemisphere, headed for a destination two and a half thousand miles away. Put like that, it sounds foolhardy!

Although the Pontiac had been running well for the last four days, there was a nagging concern at the back of my mind. Ben had telephoned me from Sacramento when we reached Mojave to tell me that he had left a quart can of engine oil in the trunk of the car. "Keep checking the engine oil level", he said. "It's likely that you'll need to top it up." Did he know something I didn't? Was there a likely problem with our motor? Checking the oil level had been easy – the dipstick, a four foot flexible wand that reached down into the bowels of the vast engine, was easy to locate. I checked the level and it seemed just about OK. But I had noticed that the oil pressure gauge always flickered around maximum, just inside the red zone. Was this a good sign, or a bad sign?

Finding where to insert the oil was more difficult, and a careful examination of the engine block located two possibilities, in neither of which I had much confidence. I read the Pontiac Grande Ville owner's handbook, and this turned out to be a mine of fascinating diagrams, statistics and helpful advice. The most relevant section to our desert journey was a thoughtful piece, helpfully illustrated with diagrams of ropes, pulleys and planks, on how to extricate the two and a half ton vehicle should we become stuck in sand. As for oil, the book made vague references to topping up the engine oil, but the location of the oil filler cap remained shrouded in mystery. This must have been classified information, available only on a 'need to know' basis. Or perhaps the Pontiac company assumed it was obvious to even the most mechanically challenged simpleton. I clearly fell into the sub-simpleton bracket – mechanical moron perhaps – who must remain in ignorance.

Deciding to err on the side of caution, I kept the can of oil in the trunk and drove halfway across the continent with one eye on the road, one on the passing landscape and the other on the oil pressure light. The wisdom of the decision was revealed at the end of our journey – I had been within a whisker of pouring my engine oil into either the brake fluid reservoir or the automatic transmission system.

Chapter 7

The wind had died down during the night, and we left Tucumcari under friendly skies. Our route guide book told us that the fifteen mile section of Route 66 between here and the town of Glenrio on the Texas border was "suitable for 4x4's". Reading between the lines, we assumed that this was code for "conditions totally unsuitable for normal vehicles". This invoked visions of deeply rutted unpaved roads and rugged off-road terrain. Mindful of earlier bone-shaking experience in the Mojave desert, and out of respect for the fact that we still had many miles to go in a thirty year old borrowed vehicle, we cautiously decided that we ought to use the freeway for this small section to the Texas border.

This was obviously a cunning ruse to keep us out of the area lest we spoil it, because we later learned that we had bypassed what was, by all accounts, a peaceful and attractive corner of New Mexico, replete with high prairie flora and fauna. It was an idyllic spot where deer and sundry unidentified furry mammals emerged curiously and fearlessly from flower-strewn meadows to inspect the rare human visitors. Scurrying roadrunners, the iconic state bird of New Mexico, outran passing vehicles. These curious running birds, members of the cuckoo family, steer with their tail like an aeroplane and can reach almost twenty miles an hour. Even more remarkable, they are reputed to be able to chase and catch rattlesnakes, and eat them.

The landscape in these parts was benign in comparison with the harshness of the arid deserts of Arizona and much of New Mexico. Unnoticed by us in the gathering twilight of the previous evening, desert had given way to prairie somewhere around Tucumcari, a vast grassy prairie which started in the easternmost part of New Mexico and extended across the entire hundred and eighty mile width of the Texas panhandle. Lying at an altitude of around three thousand feet, the Texas panhandle forms the southernmost part of the Great Plains, a vast area stretching down from the Canadian border to Texas. The entire Great Plains area has been experiencing a crisis of depopulation, and both the rural areas and most of the towns have suffered severe population drops in the last fifty years. The causes of the malaise are complex, but at the heart of the problem lies the economics of agriculture. Farms have become bigger and have been mechanized, and the panoply of jobs supporting local agriculture has declined. Faced with a lack of local jobs, the young people moved away to the big cities.

The corridor of the Great Plains through which we were driving – crossing eastern New Mexico, northern Texas and western Oklahoma – had suffered a cruel double whammy, hit by the general decline of the Great Plains and impacted also by the bypassing of Route 66 by the new freeway and the loss of the service jobs associated with Route 66. Some towns were clinging to life, others had given up the unequal struggle. We slipped off the highway and stopped in Glenrio, a small town on the edge of Texas, where every building was derelict and empty. The shattered motel proclaimed the First (and Last) Motel in Texas. A derelict car stood on the forecourt of the abandoned gasoline station. The only sign of life was a work party of a power utility company who had stopped by for an extended mid-morning break. Our unexpected arrival in town galvanized them back into reluctant activity.

We continued east across the wide Texas plain, the road stretching away in front of us as straight as an arrow. A chance meeting with an oncoming vehicle was a rarity and stopping in the highway to take photographs was no problem at all, safe in the knowledge that no vehicles were visible to either the front or the rear horizon. With a regularity of every couple of miles or so we would pass a T-junction, the narrow intersecting road, straight as a ruler, marching purposely south towards the distant horizon to some mysterious unnamed destination.

Two towns vie for the honour of being the midpoint of Route 66 – Adrian and Vega – and to be absolutely impartial we stopped at both, at Adrian to visit the Midpoint Café and at Vega to take on gasoline. Both have the hallmark of Texas panhandle towns, a couple of huge grain elevators rising like stumps from the prairie, providing a navigation aid for travellers, visible from miles around. Navigation across a prairie totally lacking in distinguishing natural features was a problem for the early nineteenth century pioneers in their slow moving covered wagons, so these intrepid travellers set up a succession of wooden marker stakes across the landscape – still in place today – and called the area the 'staked plains'. Even the railroad, laid down in the latter half of the nineteenth century, has been decommissioned in these parts, and the abandoned track-bed closely shadowed the road like a silent ghost.

In practice, the landscape of the Great Plains area we were passing through was progressively changing, albeit so slowly as to be imperceptible. In the west of Texas, the prairie was a vast stretch of parched grassland, but this gradually greened up until, by the time we reached Oklahoma, it was decidedly lush. Travelling from west to east, occasional cultivated fields appeared, then the occasional paddock of horses and a few cattle, finally giving way to fully fledged farms. All the way, the Texas trademark windmills dotted the landscape, fragile looking structures generating a little electricity or pumping water for isolated farmsteads.

Our map told us that this was the way to Amarillo, the only major town in the Texas panhandle area. We tra-la-la'd into the parking lot of the edge-of-town shopping mall. In Britain, Amarillo has long been famous for the catchy lyrics of Tony Christie's popular hit song, "Is this the way to Amarillo?" Strangely, this song was unknown in Amarillo. Possibly singing along with Burl Ives' 'Bringing in the sheaves' was more the local style. But it wasn't the charms of sweet Marie waiting for us which had drawn us to Amarillo. We had been attracted by the prospect of shopping in the biggest textiles store east of California, a Mecca for stitchers throughout the Great Plains. As we looked round the parking lot, it was gratifying to note that in one significant respect Texas had today more than met its match - our car, our vast blue and white behemoth with the California license plates, was by a considerable margin the biggest car in town!

In Texas, Amarillo is famous as the home of the Big American Steak Ranch, a renowned eatery and shrine to overindulgence where steak lovers can take the "Seventy-two ounce steak challenge." This requires the contestant to consume, in less than an hour, a four-and-a-half pound slab of prime Texas beef, which probably amounts to just a little less than half a cow. Survivors of the challenge get to eat free. It was midday, but somehow we managed to eschew the lure of the local steaks and took advantage of more healthy eating options to buy a 'Greek salad-to-go' from a delicatessen. It was fortunate that we decided to share one between us. True to Texan stereotype, it was big enough to feed a small army for a week and provided us with sustaining snacks for several days.

Every town in America seemed to promote itself around its own unique selling point. For example, we once passed through a small town in Massachusetts which made the proud claim to be the 'Plastics Extrusions Capital of New England'. One of my favourites was the town of Beaver in Oklahoma, which claimed to be the 'Cow Chip Throwing Capital of the World' and home of the annual Cow Chip Throwing World Championships. Flinging crumbling wads of dried bovine excrement discus-style may not yet have been endorsed by the International Olympic Committee, but as least it had brought pride and prosperity to this enterprising town.

Amarillo's claim was 'World Capital for Helium'. We weren't in town long enough to learn whether this was excavated from the local helium mines or produced in the local hog manure processing plant. From observation, Amarillo might also have had a reasonable chance of winning the accolade of 'Home of the World's Biggest Car Wrecker Yard'. But there was one title which Amarillo wasn't pitching for, and it didn't rate a mention in any of the tourist literature or civic promotions. For much of the Cold War period, Amarillo was home to the final assembly plant for all the USA's nuclear weapons, probably guaranteeing the town the position as number one target for any nuclear strike.

It seemed that the town's good folk must still be sheltering in bunkers somewhere as we drove out of town along wide deserted boulevards. Continuing eastwards from Amarillo, the panhandle landscape unrolled as before. We passed through Conway (with its inevitable grain elevator) and turned off the highway to visit 'Bug Ranch'. Beside the road, a line of multicoloured VW Beetles protruded from the earth at an angle of sixty degrees, buried nose downwards and covered in graffiti. I'm not sure what subtle statement the owner of this art-form was intending to make, perhaps something on the lines, 'Whatever you can do, I can do too'. 'Bug Ranch' was created as a riposte to a wealthy eccentric called Stanley Marsh 3 who in 1974 created the celebrated 'Cadillac Ranch' on the same principle, on the other side of Amarillo. There, the rear ends of ten graffiti-decorated classic Cadillacs thrust skywards from the Texas dirt, perfectly aligned and poised, like a latter day Stonehenge or a druidic temple to the twentieth century automobile god. The artistic possibilities are endless, and perhaps one day an enigmatic 'Mondeo Ranch' will rise beside England's Great North Road, vying with the 'Angel of the North' for the attention of passing travellers.

Nearing the tiny community of Groom, the 'Tallest Cross in the Western Hemisphere' soared above the prairie. This monument was erected in a field as a statement of faith by Steve Thomas, a devout local farmer. The nineteen storey gleaming white edifice, which is visible to travellers on both Route 66 and the nearby freeway from miles around, rises a hundred and ninety feet, weighs one thousand two hundred and fifty tons, contains seventy five tons of steel, and was worked on by a hundred welders for eight months at its fabrication site forty miles away. It is now maintained by 'The Cross of Our Lord Jesus Ministries', who were happy to provide visitors with this statistical data together with Bible quotations about the Christian teaching on salvation. We inspected the group of bronze sculptures depicting Jesus' journey to the cross which were clustered in the shadow of the great cross, read the explanatory plaques and checked out the replica of the empty tomb which had been constructed near the base. It was a deeply impressive location and we were the only visitors around.

On leaving the parking lot and rejoining the road, we spied a sign for Blessed Mary's Tex-Mex Restaurant. We felt we must pay it a visit. As we entered the café, the only customers, four elderly 'good ol' boys' in baseball caps who were sitting motionless round a table looking into empty coffee cups, turned and watched solemnly and wordlessly as we made our way to a table. As we progressed across the room, we noticed that the proprietor, an elderly gentleman, lay fast asleep in a horizontally reclined dentist's chair just a couple of feet above floor level. His buddies didn't allow him to continue the sleep of the just. One of them grunted, "Hey Jim, you've got customers!"

The dozen tables in the café were each named for one of the first disciples, and we sat down at 'James the son of Zebedee'. It took a second grunt and a nudge to reach the somnolent Jim. Unexpectedly roused from his nap, he gradually stirred himself into life, found his walking stick and swayed across the room towards us, steadying himself on the other tables as he passed them. Ours was a simple order – two coffees, please – and he started on the return journey to the coffee machine. I had noticed that the filter coffee jug on the stove had just a fraction of an inch of coffee remaining in the bottom, so unwisely asked if he would be making fresh coffee. Jim looked puzzled. "It was good enough for them", he responded, jerking his head in the direction of the good ol' boys sitting at 'Matthew the Tax Collector'. Suffice to say that I was served the dregs, and Lois was served a cup of hot water which had made a quick pass over the filter of spent grains.

By now fully awake, Jim came and sat at an adjacent table, 'Simon the Zealot' I think. He was a friendly and concerned host, and plied us with questions, the sort of questions every restaurant owner normally asks his guests.

Had we been to the Cross?
Had Mel Gibson's film 'The Passion of the Christ' been released in England?
Had we seen it and what was our opinion of it?
Did we know that the Baptists were founded by a woman in the fifteenth century?
Had we seen the replica of the Turin shroud over at the Cross? The fact that we had to answer no to this last question shocked him and he became animated.
Hadn't the attendants directed our attention to it? We hadn't seen any attendants.

Clearly the shroud was his passion. Remarkable things had happened at that shroud and also at his café. A nine year old girl had clearly seen an image on the replica shroud as her father photographed it, and she had come into his café face aglow, moving as if on a cloud. Someone else had been healed in the café. Jim himself had been awakened at four thirty in the morning by an audible voice which instructed him to buy the café and turn it over to Mary. He had been sixty six at the time and planning a quiet retirement. Now all the takings of the café were handed over to Mary – "well, to Jesus, I suppose." Last year all the takings were given to the work of the Cross. How much did we owe him for our coffees? "Nothing, but just make a gift when you go out. But can I make you any food? Hamburgers, burritos or enchiladas, perhaps?" We suddenly realized we really ought to be on our way. We made our gift and slipped away.

A few miles down the road we passed through McLean, home of the 'Devil's Rope Museum'. In true Texan style, this museum claims to be the 'largest barbed wire museum in the world' – it may also be the only barbed wire museum in the world – and it was a minor disappointment to find that it had closed at four o'clock. (We passed though McLean at four twenty.) Collecting strands of barbed wire is an exciting hobby in these parts and more than two thousand different variants have been identified. Apparently, it's easy to get hooked on barbed wire; in fact, it's quite catching.

Invented by Joseph Glidden in the 1860s, barbed wire is credited by enthusiasts as being the one most significant reason why the west was won. The claim was, "Barbed wire gave control of the land, and windmills made it habitable." But it was a controversial invention. Landowners built barbed wire fences in order to protect crops and livestock. Open range grazers thought that their livelihoods would be destroyed. Cattle drovers were worried that their route to the Kansas markets would be blocked. Religious groups called it "The Devil's Rope", on account of the injuries barbed wire caused, and demanded its removal. Tempers were raised, violence flared, and many died before the Fence Cutter Wars ended.

Arriving at our hotel in the small town of Shamrock, we stepped out of the car into the teeth of a moderate hurricane and wrestled energetically with the Pontiac's convertible top against the howling gale. The hotel clerk, who had given up the bright lights and attractions of Los Angeles to return to her home town, told us cheerfully that it was always windy in this part of Texas. The only question to be asked was, how strong the wind?

'God blew with his winds and they were scattered' was the inscription on the victory medals which were struck by the Queen of England to mark the defeat of the Spanish Armada. The story of settlement of the Texas panhandle might have been summed up, 'God blew with his winds and men went elsewhere instead.' These persistent driving winds well illustrated why the panhandle was never a coveted destination for westward thrusting pioneers. The history of American expansion recorded that, even as the final shots of the Civil War faded away across now silent battlefields, settlers were already preparing to head out towards every far-flung western point of the continent; barring, of course, the despised panhandle. To aspire to the panhandle seemed the very height of insanity. This was the insanity induced in sober men and women by the year-round roaring gale. This was the insanity of cruel winter when vicious wind-borne hail and sleet would well nigh cut a man or a mule in two. This was the insanity of roaming the untamed prairie, lost and at the mercy of the merciless sun and the stinging dust carried in the relentless whining wind. Everyone knew the Texas panhandle was a God-forsaken place.

But despite all this, the citizens of Shamrock turned out to be a well adjusted and cheerful lot. Shamrock was a cross-roads town, and the Route 66 road through the town was trail of dereliction and abandoned ironmongery. In the garden of one forsaken home a flock of white goats gambolled atop the auto wrecks. The intersecting street had been more successful in clinging to life, and was host to the town library, motels, the supermarket, a couple of gasoline stations and McDonalds restaurant.

At the cross-roads stood the restored Conoco service station and the 'U-Drop In' café, housed in a wonderfully restored 1930s art deco building of beige and green tiles with soaring towers at either end. Elegantly pillared concrete canopies reached out over the filling-station forecourt, and atop the Conoco tower what looked like a twelve foot sculpture of an empty flower vase thrust skyward. This splendid edifice would be an eye catcher anywhere, but in Shamrock it was truly an architectural wonder. Our determination to eat at the 'U-Drop In' café was sadly frustrated. We peered through the window at the neatly arranged tables and chairs, but it was apparently one of those cafés which closed at meal times.

The town certainly seemed to be making the most of its Irish roots, positioning itself as a little piece of the emerald isle set down in a corner of Texas – Shamrock boasted the Blarney Motel, the Irish Motel, a St Patrick's Day Parade, a fragment of the true Blarney Stone mounted on a pillar, and a 'Welcome' sign featuring a cheerful leering leprechaun. But a quick delve below the surface showed that the town's historical link with the land of the shamrock was – a sham, or extremely tenuous to say the least. In 1890, a homesick Irish shepherd applied to open a post office at his lonely homestead six miles to the north. The name Shamrock was accepted by postal officials, but the post office never opened, probably because his homestead burned down the same year. What became of the Irishman isn't recorded.

Twelve years later in August 1902, the present town was founded and its original name was Wheeler. But the Chicago, Rock Island and Gulf Railway came to town at exactly the same time and they named their train stop 'Shamrock'! It was a few years later that the town followed suit and became incorporated as Shamrock. It was a smart move – Shamrock is definitely a much friendlier name than Wheeler. And who knows, the luck of the Irish and the invocation of St Patrick may have contributed to the survival, if not the prosperity, of the little community of Shamrock.

No service today, Newkirk, New Mexico

Long since checked out, Route 66

On the trail in New Mexico

'Art Deco'-style Conoco filling station, Shamrock, Texas

Going nowhere, Shamrock, Texas

Old Round Barn of Arcadia, Oklahoma

Not open for business, Galena, Kansas

Drive-in movie theatre, Carthage, Missouri

Chapter 8

We left Shamrock in a light morning breeze and soon crossed the border into Oklahoma. Since leaving Shamrock, we had become aware of a new phenomenon – wildlife! Throughout the hot arid desert and the parched high plains we had not noticed any birds or animals. They must have been hiding out there somewhere, but we just didn't see them. But as we drove across the final stretches of the Texas panhandle and on into Oklahoma, life had gradually begun to reassert itself. Small birds fluttered up from the roadside verges and darted in front of the car. Nondescript brown birds, birds in red, blue, yellow hues, an earthbound kiwi-like bird. Our favourite was an elegant pink and orange long-tailed bird which would soar from the bushes as we passed. This, we learned, was the Scissor-Tailed Flycatcher, a handsome bird and the state bird of Oklahoma. Ponderous black crows wheeled overhead. Squashed pelts of unidentified furry creatures which hadn't been sufficiently agile adhered to the road surface with pathetic regularity. A tortoise, horny head stretching forward like a sprinter and little leathery hind legs propelling it purposefully forward, crossed the road with a surprising turn of speed. A couple of bashful armadillos lurked shyly in the shadow of a fence.

Unfortunately, human life didn't seem to have coped so well. We passed through a succession of sad and crumbling townships. Texola, the first town in Oklahoma, a veritable ghost town; Erick, still clinging to a semblance of normality, where only every third house showed any signs of occupation, others were derelict and yet others were boarded up as if in imminent expectation of an approaching hurricane. At times the countryside looked as if the populace had just given up the unequal struggle and walked away. In fields and gardens lay abandoned rusting cars, broken tractors and ancient agricultural machinery. Many of those who fled in the 1930s dust-bowl era had never returned, and increasing farm mechanization meant that a farm which had at one time provided work for a whole community could now be managed by one man and a dog. The loss of direct agricultural jobs also resulted in a steep decline in service jobs needed to support the people in the farming sector and their families – storekeepers, blacksmiths, teachers, merchants. Most communities in the region now have a lower population than they did a hundred years ago, and public services are increasingly stretched by the decline in numbers and the ageing of the population.

Looking at the flat green landscape, it was difficult to visualize the climatic conditions which turned it into an arid dust bowl, and impossible to know whether such a disaster could happen again in the future. But it was probable then that economic mismanagement had made a decisive contribution to the unfolding human tragedy. When the people were down but not out, reeling from the effects of several years' drought which had decimated the meagre harvests of their homesteads, and struggling to cope with the wind-borne clouds of fine red dust which engulfed the land and penetrated every nook and cranny, it was the banks which put the boot in. Bereft of income, the farmers were already heavily in debt to the banks. The banks foreclosed on the debts and took possession of the farms, initially retaining the homesteaders as tenant farmers. Finally, in a twentieth century equivalent of the highland clearances, the banks drove the tenants from the land to create vast aggregated factory farms. It was not sheep, but cotton, to which these huge units were put. In the event, cotton proved to be an unsuitable crop for this environment and in due course these units failed. But the human damage had been done and many thousands had been dispossessed. The ranking position in American demonology historically held by banks, feared and despised by pioneering people for their insensitivity and use of power without accountability, was secure. It was not until very recent years that Americans were sufficiently weaned from their suspicion of banks to allow them to operate across state boundaries. Even now, the American psyche carries a lurking distrust of the banking system.

But Oklahomans are proud of the contribution they have made to human well being. The parking meter was invented and first installed in Oklahoma in 1935. The supermarket shopping cart was invented by an Oklahoman. Oklahoma-born Will Rogers, famous Broadway and movie star of the 1920s and 1930s era, broadcaster and columnist, was born a Cherokee Indian in 1879 and was a cowboy before he became a national figure. We passed through the small town of Weatherford where a life size statue honours Astronaut Thomas Stafford, a local boy who commanded Apollo Ten in May 1969 and made the first independent flight of the lunar module towards the surface of the moon. A less well known pair of Oklahoman high flyers was a man and his wife in Ponca who were carried aloft in their house by a tornado. The walls and roof were blown away. But the floor remained in place and eventually glided downward, setting the couple safely back on the ground.

Through much of the nineteenth century, Oklahoma was known as Indian Territory and was the designated homeland of the so-called 'Five Civilised Tribes' - the Creeks, Cherokees, Choctaws, Chickasaws and Seminoles. Not that this territory had been their ancestral home lands. Many had come there as a result of Federal government policies of forced removals to the designated Indian Territory. The infamous 'Trail of Tears' was the final Cherokee migration in 1838 from Tennessee, Georgia and the Carolinas to the designated 'Cherokee Nation' in what is now north-eastern Oklahoma. The Seminole, who had been accused of helping and sheltering runaway slaves, were forcibly migrated from the south east states after a series of military actions known as the Seminole Wars. Indian Territory became an administrative entity organised into counties along tribal lines, and at that time the Native Americans believed this territory was theirs by treaty "as long as grass grows and water runs."

They were wrong. European settlers and homesteaders couldn't wait to get their hands on it. It was opened to settlers in a 'Land Rush' in 1889. On 22 April 1889, the first day homesteading was permitted, fifty thousand people swarmed into the area at the signal of the noon starting gun, claiming plots of land by grabbing the stakes which marked out each plot. A few of them jumped the gun and sneaked in to claim land before the official start. These cheaters became known as 'Sooners', a name which has stuck as the nickname for Oklahomans. Today, many of the quarter of a million Native Americans living in Oklahoma are descended from the sixty seven tribes who made up the population of Indian

Territory, and Oklahoma has a higher Native American population than any other American state.

We made a stop at Clinton and visited the Route 66 museum. This was the third such museum we had visited – Barstow in California, Kingman in Arizona and now Clinton, Oklahoma. Each one was different in its own way. Barstow was cheerful and folksy in an amateurish sort of way, stuffed with memorabilia and photos. Kingman was professionally presented, with story boards and exhibits that majored on the social history and human stories of the travellers. Clinton was slick and commercial, and centred on the engineering and construction aspects of the route. Taken together, all angles of Route 66 were well covered! Opposite the Clinton museum, we lunched on potato soup and oyster crackers at the restaurant attached to the Trade Winds Motel, suitably impressed by the Motel's amazing claim to fame – Elvis once slept here.

As we continued on our way across Oklahoma, the landscape visibly cheered up. A landscape which had started off as green, flat and featureless gradually gave way to a green and rolling English-style countryside, with wooded hills, farms and cultivated fields. The towns we passed through became busier and more prosperous as the miles rolled by, and by the time we reached the outskirts of Oklahoma City, normal service had been resumed. Bustling brash and prosperous America had reasserted itself.

It had been our intention to continue to follow the course of the old Route 66 through the centre of downtown Oklahoma City, but the route signage we were following disappeared at a busy and complex intersection. We made an instantaneous decision – the wrong one, inevitably – and found ourselves swept unwillingly onto the engirdling city beltway. It was the early stages of the evening rush hour, and this was al fresco motoring at its worst. Sandwiched between thunderous high sided trucks on either side, and pursued by a roaring pack of juggernauts a few feet behind our tail, we suddenly felt extremely vulnerable and aware of our mortality. Having driven almost halfway across a continent, mostly on benign two lane roads where frequently the sight of another vehicle had been a cause for comment, this was a sudden shock to the system. Drawn along in the roaring vortex, we caught momentary glimpses between the trucks of high rise downtown office towers, warehouses, railroad yards, bridges and flyovers, until we were eventually spewed out, like Jonah from the whale, onto the sudden tranquillity of the old Route 66 to the north east of Oklahoma City.

Luxuriating in this new found sense of peace, we pulled off the highway opposite a large red circular building just outside the small community of Arcadia. Celebrated as one of the ancient wonders of the world of Route 66, this was the famous red Round Barn of Arcadia, a 'must see' attraction for travellers along the adjacent highway. Apparently people came from far and wide to admire it. There was even a folk song entitled "That Old Round Barn in Arcadia". We went inside and met Butch, the resident curator, a serious and slow talking Oklahoman with a deep passion for round barns. Butch showed us photographs and news clippings of other round barns in various US States, but his was apparently the only one in the State of Oklahoma. He became almost animated when he discovered we were from England. Were we from the north of England? He had heard a rumour that there might be a round barn in the north of England, a round barn with a bell on top of it. Sadly we were unable to confirm this, and research back home in England has so far been unable to track one down.

The reason why these barns were built circular was somewhat of a mystery. One theory was that such barns were first constructed by members of the Shakers sect, and that they were built round so as to provide no corners where the devil could hide. Another less supernatural theory was that they were built round so that they could better withstand tornados. I have my own theory, based on my sketchy knowledge of agricultural archaeology, which is that the shape derived from threshing barns where oxen yoked to a beam walked in perpetual circles to turn a spindle which drove grinding machinery – a sort of animal-powered windmill.

The Arcadia round barn was built in 1898, but had been brought back from the brink of decay more recently by a dedicated team of enthusiasts. Sixty feet in diameter and forty five feet high, the building comprised two levels. The upper level offered a superb circular function room with a fine wooden floor, and it could be hired for weddings, parties, receptions, bar mitzvahs, meetings and country dancing. The only thing it was not suitable for, Butch told us, was square dances – clearly a well used joke. The lower level was dedicated to the display of historical information and souvenir sales.

Included in the display area was just a tiny part of the brick collection of the late Luther Robison, the prime mover of the round barn preservation project. Luther was also a founder member of the International Brick Collectors Association (IBCA), and apparently his home contained an extensive collection of historic bricks from different manufacturers across Oklahoma, the USA and presumably the rest of the world too. The most highly prized examples were nineteenth century bricks imprinted with the name of the brickyard and the suffix IT – for Indian Territory. I had not previously been aware of this hobby. 'Brick Journal', the

IBCA's thrice yearly publication, contained exciting features such as 'My favourite brick - Pictures of members holding that special brick.' It was clearly an addictive hobby, but no doubt Luther's wife wished he had taken up stamp collecting instead. The information display didn't mention whether Luther also collected barbed wire.

That evening we lodged in Chandler, Oklahoma, at the Lincoln Motel. This was a 1939 original motel where the accommodation was in two rows of cosy red wooden semi-detached bungalows, each with a green bench outside and an individual American flag snapping in the breeze. Even the bed linen - although neat and clean - looked 1939 vintage. Founded soon after the 1889 Land Rush, Chandler became one of Oklahoma's oil boom towns and, as county seat of Lincoln County, the location of the courthouse and jail. The self-styled 'Pecan Capital of the World', Chandler was archetypal small town America, with a single Main Street of flat fronted stores and cars parked echelon style facing the sidewalk. We ate well at Granny's Country Kitchen restaurant and I don't think there was a pecan in sight. After checking out what there was to do in Chandler – answer, nothing – we retired early to our room to watch television.

Incidentally, it would seem that Chandler has a fight on its hands, as at least two other towns, Albany in Georgia and Brunswick in Missouri, also lay claim to the distinction of 'Pecan Capital of the World.' I doubt whether Chandler would win – it seemed far too laid back for that – but there is probably some other world title left to which it could aspire. But a quick search of the Internet showed that most worthwhile titles have already been claimed. The 'Football Capital of the World' – no it's not Liverpool or Manchester, and it's not Milan or Madrid – is Ada, Ohio, a town of five thousand people which has a factory which makes footballs.

The 'Broccoli Capital of the World' is Greenfield, California, and El Reno, Oklahoma, is the 'Onion Fried Burger Capital of the World'. The title 'Spinach Capital of the World' is hotly disputed by both Alma, Arkansas, and Crystal City, Texas. McLean, Texas, seems to be complacently unaware that La Crosse, Kansas, is calling itself the 'Barbed Wire Capital of the World'. And enigmatically, Mannford, Oklahoma, is the 'Striper Capital of the World'.

Inside our cosy cabin we settled down to watch the offering from a local TV station, a good British film, Notting Hill, starring Hugh Grant. The continuity of the film was disrupted almost every five minutes by commercial breaks. A few years ago these would have been highlighting the savage price cuts down at the local Chevrolet franchise, with enticing shots of the forecourt festooned with tacky tinsel streamers in red, white and blue; or they would be extolling the virtues of a particularly vicious looking set of kitchen knives at a deeply discounted forty-nine dollars ninety-nine cents. But now they all seemed to be promoting various prescription drugs, efficacious for such ailments as acne, allergies and depression. Invariably, and no doubt for legal reasons to head off possible claims, the advertisements reeled off lists of scary possible side effects – I recall that these included sexual dysfunction, seizures and blackouts. I think I'd prefer to just stick with the acne!

Chapter 9

In the morning we stopped in at the Chandler bakery and café to pick up coffee and cinnamon rolls for breakfast. We had clearly chanced on the social hub of the village. A group of 'good ol' boys' – five or six of them – seated round a long trestle table in the centre of the café greeted us cheerfully as we entered. As we ate our rolls, we eavesdropped as the group in the centre exchanged banter and gossiped about themselves, their buddies and their neighbours. The composition of the group was regularly changing as some left and others joined, both men and women. It was a sort of alternative town council and the gossip seemed caring, a group of buddies watching out for each other and for their neighbours. If someone had a problem in Chandler, it would soon be taken care of. As we left the café, they called after us, "Come and see us again!" So how about this for a suggestion? 'Chandler – Caring Capital of Lincoln County'. It's suitably modest, but it seems to fit.

About halfway between Oklahoma City and the border with Kansas, we passed through Tulsa. Our guide book was very complimentary about Tulsa. Apparently it was the 'Oil Capital of the World', was the nicest city in Oklahoma and had some attractive Art Deco buildings. But in Tulsa we were witnesses to a shocking piece of driving that almost resulted in the abrupt termination of our expedition. A dithering driver in a huge blue convertible, a handsome young man but obviously a stranger to the city and very uncertain of his route, suddenly braked as he unexpectedly came level with 11th Street where he was due to make a right turn. With a screech of tyres, the driver of the car behind managed heroically to stop just in time to avoid a crunching collision. He was clearly angered and shaken by such a display of crass incompetence. You've guessed it! I was that offender.

Of course, there were, as always, strongly mitigating circumstances. The fractured road surface had potholes the size of golf bunkers and craters like the lunar surface. The traffic signs for transiting traffic were woefully lacking. And we were attempting to navigate our way through the city by following, in reverse, a set of directions for a route inconsiderately full of one-way streets. We didn't see any of Tulsa's Art Deco buildings, but did notice some rather fetching intersections, flyovers and traffic lights. By the time we exited Tulsa to the east, we were ready for a little recuperative retail and coffee therapy at a WalMart store with floor area approximately the size of Rhode Island, which restored our equanimity.

Our route sliced north-eastwards across Oklahoma, frequently as straight as a die. The red fertile soil was totally concealed by the lush green of roadside verges and farm pastures. So it was both surprising and disappointing to find that as we progressed towards the distant reaches of Oklahoma, away from the economic influence of Oklahoma City, the towns grew noticeably poorer, the shattered and shuttered commercial premises returned, and quirky motels long closed to visitors stood forlornly around overgrown courtyards beside the highway. Most towns – and this was something characteristic of 'old west' towns – had one or more 'bail bond' lawyers on Main Street, prominently promoting their 'get out of jail quick' services. I'm sure this was a cultural throwback to more lawless days rather than any reflection on the rectitude of the current citizens. The only parallel in England is with the adverts for the services of criminal lawyers, should you be unlucky enough to be charged with burglary, robbery or murder, placed in the Millwall football fan magazine.

We left Oklahoma and entered the State of Kansas close to the town of Baxter Springs, the 'First Cowtown in Kansas'. We threaded our way through the streets and round the town square of this shabby but proud little town. Clearly Baxter Springs is searching for a new role, having already concluded four careers since it was founded less than a hundred and fifty years ago. Baxter Springs was firstly a military fort set up to protect the old West from hostile Indians and to supply troops to escort wagon trains through the dangerous Indian Territory. During the Civil War it hosted regiments of the Kansas Indian Home Guard and the 1st Kansas Colored Troops, and was the site of the Baxter Springs Massacre when Confederate guerrillas struck in October 1863. Over 100 Union troops in Baxter Springs, many of them freed slaves, were killed or injured in this raid, but the attacking guerrillas eventually fled in alarm when the fort fired its big gun.

After this military period, the level of local mayhem stepped up a notch as Baxter Springs entered on its second career, becoming known as one of the wildest cowtowns of the West. For cowboys, driving their herds of cattle northward from Texas to the markets of Missouri and the Midwest, this was the first town they came to after crossing

Indian Territory and three or four months on the trail. It became a rip-roaring hell-raising saloon town, a hotbed of violence fuelled by gambling and drink. The outlaw Jesse James famously robbed the town bank here and, Robin Hood-style, ambushed and disarmed the pursuing sheriff's posse.

Economic ruin threatened when the railroads came to Texas and the cowboys no longer came to town. Baxter Springs cleverly 'discovered' that the local mineral springs had wonderful health-giving properties and for a while reinvented itself – its third career - as a famous health spa. Then lead and zinc were discovered in this corner of Kansas, and Baxter Springs became a booming business centre, a fourth career. Since the demise of mining, Baxter Springs has been looking for a new vocation. The only contribution we were able to make to the regeneration of the local economy was to purchase a tank of gasoline.

The weather forecast as we left Oklahoma that morning had given dire warnings of storms ahead and a reminder of the onset of the tornado season. The newspapers were carrying reports of vehicles being swept off bridges by flash floods in neighbouring Arkansas, and of campers in Oklahoma being swept away by floodwaters. We saw none of this and motored along all day, open top, cocooned in a benign microclimate of sunshine and warmth, but as we crossed Kansas, it was clear from the awash roads and verges that a violent storm had passed through the area just a few minutes before our arrival. This small corner of Kansas looked like a green and pleasant part of the world with streams, meadows and woods. We stopped at the 1920s era general store near the small community of Riverton where the proprietor told us of Route 66 travellers from all over the world who had visited his store – England, Egypt and Japan were mentioned. Earlier, at Adrian, Texas, we had been told about a Swiss man who had passed through the previous day, cycling the length of Route 66. Someone else told us about the young Frenchman on rollerblades doing the same thing. Strangely, despite all these apocryphal stories, we never actually met anyone else who was travelling the length of Route 66 during the whole of our journey.

The section of the Route 66 which passed through the state of Kansas was very short – less than fifteen miles – but it certainly made up in interest what it lacked in length. We entered the town of Galena and made a left at the cross road in the centre of town. 'Galena' is the common name for the mineral lead sulphide, the principal ore from which lead is extracted, and an appropriate name for this mining town, or rather, former mining town. From 1873 and for the next one hundred years, Galena was the centre of the local lead mining industry, becoming well known for its history of industrial strife and violence during the dying years of the mines. Once known as the Queen City of Kansas, a hundred years ago Galena was one of the most prosperous towns west of New York.

But its population, which at its peak was around thirty thousand people, is now less than four thousand. The town, or what was left of it, was now a sad picture of resigned despair. Every second building lot appeared to have been flattened and cleared. Many – perhaps most – of the remaining commercial buildings in town were either derelict or boarded up. A fragment of tiling was all that remained of the Citizens Bank. The Palace Drug Store was long closed and Dolly's Diner probably hadn't served a burger for forty years. We left the town beside 'Hell's Half Acre', the desolate site of the redundant mining complex, crossed the railroad tracks and headed for Missouri.

We passed through the Missouri gateway town of Joplin, a lively bustling town with all the commercial trappings of modern America, and headed to nearby Carterville, a suburban backwater of faded gentility. Here we spent a frustrating hour boxing the compass as we struggled to extricate ourselves. It was almost five o'clock and raining lightly, so our well honed instincts of navigating by the direction of the sun were of no use. By the time we had passed the same junction and the same landmark for the second or the third time, frustration had been replaced by resignation. Nevertheless, we eventually succeeded in escaping the clutches of Carterville and found our way to Carthage, Missouri, where there was a goodly choice of overnight accommodation.

Carthage is a good exponent of the art of being small town Midwest America, a peaceful and respectable town of elegant houses and leafy streets, standing in contrast to its brash neighbour Joplin. We stopped in the parking lot of the only restored drive-in cinema on Route 66. On this particular week the cinema was only operating on Friday evening, which was a slight disappointment to us because to watch a drive-in movie would have been something of a novel experience. (Actually, we realized later that it *was* Friday evening, but after days on the road all had begun to blur into one continuum of days.)

At the centre of Carthage was the town square, and in the centre of the landscaped square stood the Town Hall, a handsome castle-like building of locally quarried limestone designed in a style reminiscent of a French Chateau. It must have cost a fortune to build in its day. Fronting the wide sidewalks of the town square on four sides was a desultory collection of stores housed in slightly shabby 1890s brick buildings. It was a sad indictment of what has happened to many American downtown areas, with the growth of out-of-town malls and shopping centres. One could imagine the equivalent in a European city, with bustling pavement cafés and coffee shops, streams of apron clad waiters scurrying between tables with trays of foaming beer, and diners leisurely perusing the menu card. Even the Carthage Deli on the corner had closed at five o'clock. It was six o'clock on a Friday evening and we were the only folks in sight.

For the first time since Albuquerque, New Mexico, we had a number of alternative choices as to where we could eat that night. We chose the Sirloin Stockade, attracted by the 'eat as much as you like' sea-food buffet which was on offer on Friday evenings. The restaurant had a very loose definition of 'sea-food', which apparently included such exotic sea creatures as chicken, pizza and pasta. Maybe the local citizenry had only a vague concept of the sea. After all, Carthage, Missouri, was about as far away from the ocean as it was possible to be in America.

Clearly the Sirloin Stockade was a very popular eatery, well patronized by the locals who were there in groups of friends and extended families. It all made compelling people watching. The food was good. Diners were loading their plates with steaming mounds of fried clams, fried shrimps, fried catfish and fried chicken, and then repeating the exercise to replenish their plates. The staff members were working very hard to keep the servery restocked. The heaped mounds on the diners' plates tended to reflect the figures of the diners, a startling proportion of the clientele being severely obese. Once again it was obvious that flab is no respecter of age, gender and race. The availability of such feasts was clearly an irresistible temptation for many. But I couldn't claim any moral high ground – when it comes to food I can resist anything but temptation.

During the night, the heavens opened. Thunder crackled, lightening flashed and the rain poured down in torrents. Across the darkened courtyard we could see it bouncing off the sidewalk and spreading black across the tarmac, and we wondered nervously how our Pontiac was coping. The answer was clear in the morning – not very well, actually. The canvas top had proved to be remarkably impervious, but the flood waters had cascaded in through the wide gap between the ill-fitting side window and the rear window. The rear floor well, behind the front seats, was awash with water. Vigorous baling out operations were required and several applications of the hotel's full complement of fluffy bath towels were needed to absorb the deluge.

When the inundation had been repelled, we repaired to the Carthage Deli in the town square for breakfast. We had noticed this eatery the previous night and made a mental note that it would make a suitable breakfast stop. The Deli was a 1950s themed establishment, bright, fun and cheerful, which had been serving Carthage for a quarter of a century. Specialities of the house included such mysteries as Reuben's, subs, French dips, smoothies, malts and ice-cream sodas. Seated in a comfy leather booth between a large railroad crossing warning bell and a full-size DX Boron gasoline pump, we ate home cooked muffins and scrambled eggs. We were the Deli's first – and perhaps only – breakfast customers this Saturday morning. It was probable that most other folks in town were sleeping off their previous evening's excesses at the Sirloin Stockade.

As we left the Deli, flower and vegetable sellers were setting up their tables beside the square in readiness for the Saturday Farmers' Market. Perhaps I had been hasty to judgment, and there was life in the old downtown yet.

A memorial on the corner of the square honoured the men in grey and the men in blue who fought in the Battle of Carthage on the fifth of July 1861. The town of Carthage was proud of its historic link with the civil war. A troop of four thousand Missouri State Guards led by Governor Jackson of Missouri, who was intent on seceding to the rebel Confederate states, was intercepted at Carthage by a Union force of one thousand Missouri Volunteers led by Colonel Sigel. The larger Confederate force had cunningly inveigled the smaller Union force, which was encamped at Carthage, into launching an attack. The battle ebbed and flowed around Carthage all day until the Union forces retreated. The Confederates, in spite of suffering two hundred casualties, chalked it up as a great victory, although the outcome in reality was somewhat inconclusive. This tendency to see things as we want to see them was reminiscent of the enduring French view of the Battle of Trafalgar – an inconclusive engagement in which the English admiral was killed.

Chapter 10

The rain looked to be well set in for the day as we motored east across the State of Missouri. We struggled to staunch the irregular stream of rain drops which dripped onto our hands and knees, penetrating the Pontiac's soft top and seeping through the crack where the top met the windshield. We skirted the northern edge of the city of Springfield, Missouri, and turned southwards, off the old Route 66, towards Mansfield. Our destination was the Laura Ingalls Wilder homestead and museum at Rocky Ridge Farm, Mansfield, where the late author had written her best selling 'Little House' children's stories about her experiences as a child during the pioneering days of the second half of the nineteenth century. These folksy books, and the associated television series, have been much loved by a couple of generations of children; Little House in the Big Woods, Little House on the Prairie, On the Banks of Plum Creek, By the Shores of Silver Lake, The Long Winter, Little Town on the Prairie.

The undulating road wound through prosperous looking farmland. Ahead of us on the wet road, the sparse traffic slowed to a crawl behind a horse-drawn Amish buggy. A couple of similar buggies waited to join the main highway at an intersection as we passed. In contrast with Amish buggies which we had previously seen in Lancaster County, Pennsylvania, these buggies were open topped, and the rain-swept occupants in their black hats and black capes huddled together against the hostile elements. We had passed several Amish farmhouses on the way, unfussy rambling white clapperboard houses with barnyard and wind pump alongside. The Amish communities came over from Europe in the eighteenth and nineteenth centuries, fleeing persecution and prejudice in Europe and seeking farming land and freedom to practice their religion and way of life in the new world. They have maintained their separate and distinctive way of life ever since, eschewing the technology and fashion developments which they associate with the modern world. New-fangled developments such as electricity, telephones and motors are not for them.

Named after one of the founders of the movement, Joseph Amman, the Amish are a German-speaking pietistic group which split away from the main Anabaptist movement which formed in Switzerland and southern Germany during the Protestant Reformation in the sixteenth century. Unlike their more numerous Anabaptist cousins the Mennonites, with whom they share a common theological and European parentage and who have tended to adopt an American identity and a more outward looking world-view, the Amish have remained closed and introspective. The Amish have themselves fragmented into various sub-groupings since their migration to North America. Probably the Missouri group's refusal to use enclosed buggies was based on some principle of practical theology, a pointed statement of their disapproval of the luxury of those new-fangled enclosed buggies used by their Amish co-religionists further east.

America The Wrong Way

We joined a line of very slow moving traffic on the divided highway (dual carriageway, in British parlance) leading towards the town of Mansfield. The weight of rainfall had caused a small river beside the highway to burst its banks and the roadway was flooded. The vehicle in front of us, a large-wheeled 4X4 pick-up truck, headed into the floodwaters and emerged successfully the other side. We followed behind, taking the line which he had taken. The depth of water was certainly above the two exhaust pipes of our Pontiac, and probably above the wheels too, but we made it successfully to the other side without stalling. The police closed the road shortly after we had passed through.

That afternoon we rejoined our route and continued across Missouri. For much of the time the old Route 66 ran along the frontage road adjacent to the new freeway, and at other times the old road no longer existed and the only option was to travel on the freeway. Compared with much of the isolated and empty terrain we had passed through in recent days, Missouri was developed and populated territory. All the strident trappings of modern America ranged themselves beside the freeway – car franchises, tire and muffler outlets, timber depots, fast food restaurants and motels. The visual assault of the roadside billboards provided an interesting insight into the concerns of modern America. Advertisements for chiropractors, vasectomy reversals, DNA paternity tests, adult book stores, employment accident attorneys.

The fact that employment accident attorneys had replaced the 'get out of jail' bail-bond lawyers reinforced the fact that we were no longer in the 'wild west'! Realization was dawning that the interesting part of our Route 66 journey might be nearing completion. Our expectation was that the remainder of the Missouri section, and the final drive through Illinois to the lakeside at Chicago, would be boringly routine. Our overwhelming wish now was just to get on with it and get to Chicago. That afternoon we covered enough miles to put us within easy striking distance of St Louis before checking into a motel in the small community of St Clair, a railroad town founded in 1843 during the early years of westward expansion out of St Louis. And, as we had done several times before, we strolled down the street and dined at the sign of the golden arches – on healthy grilled chicken salads. We were beginning to feel like walking testimonials for McDonald's.

The next day dawned bright and breezy, the rain and clouds of the previous day just a distant memory. It was Sunday morning, and television stations were offering viewers a choice of church services. A silver bearded, silver tongued pastor was presenting a gospel which promised his listeners 'health and wealth', based on his reading of a text in the Old Testament Book of Proverbs; 'The blessing of the Lord maketh rich and addeth no sorrow with it.'

We hadn't planned to be in church today, but as we drove towards St Louis it seemed as though we must be the only people who weren't. Every community we passed had at least one church, sometimes several, elegant white clapperboard or brick structures with a slender spire, surrounded by well-filled parking lots. These were prosperous communities, within commuting distance of St Louis, set in rolling green countryside, with houses and churches set in well-manicured landscaped settings. But it had been a characteristic of communities right across America, even the poorest through which we had passed on earlier days, that God's house was frequently the most modern and well-kept building in town.

The mantra of choice is firmly etched in the American soul. In dining, the long litany of dressings – Italian, ranch, blue cheese, thousand island and the rest of them – has been ritually intoned by servers from Seattle to Savannah for generations; diners seriously consider this information, as if hearing it for the first time, before solemnly exercising their constitutional right to choose. But in matters of religion, the choices available to the faithful were legion, offering a doctrinal cafeteria of permutations and combinations. Observation showed that these ranged, alphabetically, from the Antioch Bible Church to the Zion Mennonite Fellowship, via the Hephzibah Church of Christ Apostolic and a myriad of points in between. Immersionists of an Arminian disposition were offered the Freewill Baptist Church; for immersionists with Calvinistic leanings there was the Grace Baptist Church; and for those who wished to hedge their bets there was the Grace Freewill Baptist Church.

The previous night we had with difficulty found our motel in St Clair. It took navigational geniuses to get lost in a four street town, but inevitably we had managed it. And in the morning, we had almost as much of a problem finding our way out. We made a couple of abortive forays down cul-de-sacs before hitting on the accredited Route 66 exit. Despite our earlier traumas in navigating Route 66 in reverse through the centres of Oklahoma City and Tulsa, we had decided that, as today was Sunday, even we could thread our way through the downtown of St Louis. In the event we were right – St Louis was a piece of cake. Since Route 66 was decommissioned, the original route now goes under a variety of aliases at different points. At this point it was masquerading as Highway 100. We followed Highway 100 through the green and pleasant rural Missouri countryside, past arable and diary farms, and through tranquil village communities.

But here's an interesting feature of American navigation. At no stage, never, did we see a direction sign to St Louis, and at no stage, even when we were entering the suburbs of the metropolis, did we ever see any written hint of where Highway 100 was headed. We might have been approaching Memphis, Atlanta, Nashville or any other American city. This characteristic was especially true of American freeways, very keen to tell you where you were, but very reluctant to tell you where you were going. Typical signs would say: ½ Mile to 23rd Street Exit, Next 5 Exits Nowhereville, Junction 146 for Lodging and Fuel, 2 Miles Exit Route 13 to Downtown Business Loop. But were we travelling in the right direction for St Louis? Ah, who knows? It was a mystery to us how the Americans managed to find their way to the moon! They certainly weren't following highway signs.

We rolled into St Louis and found our way to the parking lot beside Union Station. It seemed that all the folks who weren't in church that Sunday had come to Union Station. We joined the unchurched and explored this fascinating temple of creative conservation. It must have been many years since regular train services operated out of Union Station, but the booking halls and the great arched roof were still in place. Instead of degenerating into a sad and empty relic of railway archaeology, the old station had been brought back to life as a bright and lively meeting centre. The passenger areas had become a complex of shops, cafés, hotel, museums and activity areas. Where railway rolling stock once stood, and thousands of expectant migrants had embarked for a new life in the virgin west, was a tastefully landscaped indoor boating lake.

We spurned the opportunity to be flung towards the great vaulted roof harnessed to a couple of long elastic bands, and did what comes naturally at eleven o'clock in the morning – we found a coffee shop. We were agreeably surprised at the excellent coffee served by 'St Louis Coffee Roasters' - our tastes in coffee are definitely European rather than American – and Lois was moved to tell Ed, the proprietor, that his was the best coffee she had yet had in America. Ed was very clearly both a proud American patriot and a dedicated enthusiast of fine coffees, probably in that order. He accepted the acclaim with modesty, and told us that he knew as soon as he saw us that we would like his coffee! There must have been a look of European sophistication about us. Europeans always liked his coffee, he explained, but Americans frequently complained to him that his coffee wasn't like Starbucks. We were not Starbucks fans either, and it seemed to us that he should take this as a compliment, not a criticism.

Ed was keen to give us a free tutorial on the noble art of coffee roasting. Starbucks apparently were guilty of roasting their beans until they looked and tasted like charcoal. He, however, had learned his trade at the feet of a master coffee roaster in Italy, and he had now been roasting coffee beans slowly and properly, European style, for twenty years. We must have made some sort of impression on Ed, because six months after our patronage of the St Louis Coffee Roasters I checked out his company website and found there what appeared to be a reference to our visit. Ed had been extremely happy to receive our 'Best Coffee in America' accolade. It was an honour he held undisputed for at least three days - until we chanced to visit an unassuming deli in downtown Chicago's Jackson Boulevard.

St Louis was the home of two famous attractions. First and foremost, was Ted Drewe's Frozen Custard emporium, a local legend for sixty years and an institution with 'must visit' status, which of course we failed to visit. And second, was the Gateway Arch, a graceful stainless steel edifice soaring more then six hundred feet above the Mississippi waterfront area, built in honour of the movement of westward expansion which issued forth from of St Louis. Those who didn't suffer from vertigo were encouraged to judder skywards in a narrow claustrophobic contraption and enjoy the splendid panorama.

And here's a little snippet from the Cold War, which I have on good authority from a reliable informant. Before the days of cruise missiles, the flyers of America's Strategic Air Command in the 1960s were puzzled as to how they were regularly outperformed in precision bombing competitions by the crews of RAF Bomber Command. For the American crews, flying, for example, from San Diego to locate a hidden missile silo in Kansas must have been like looking for a needle in a hayfield. The secret, which can now be revealed for the first time, was that the British boys, flying down from Canada in their Vulcan bombers, accurately calibrated their target destination coordinates from the wonderfully clear all-weather radar echo provided by this vast steel structure.

Navigating only by old-fashioned maps, we homed in on the centre of downtown St Louis and were duly impressed by the city. It seemed green, clean and pleasant, with squares set around with friendly stores and offices, a place where pedestrians walked and traffic took second place. We had caught St Louis at a good time, a pleasant Sunday midday when folks were out for a stroll. But the city was rapidly starting to fill up. Groups, and then waves, of sports fans in St Louis Cardinals shirts surged towards us, spilling onto the streets. Streams of cars, bearing fans of a different allegiance, were coming from the direction of the great arch and riverside drive, and turning into the downtown area. Obviously a game was in the offing somewhere close by. Our ignorance was such that we didn't even know whether the Cardinals played baseball or football. But we carried with us a European perception of the mayhem that usually ensues when rival fans meet, and decided that the time was right for us to quit town.

After an unintended gyration of a vast public parking-lot close to the riverside and an unplanned tour of the old cotton warehouse district, we extricated ourselves from the tentacles of the St Louis road system and found a modern road bridge across the wide mud-coloured waters of the Mississippi River, just north of the famous Chain of Rocks Bridge. This mile long bridge, with a sharply angled bend in the middle, was opened in 1929 but closed to road traffic in the 1960s, and now stood as a monument to the days when engineers built bridges that looked like bridges. It was a sort of American answer to the Firth of Forth railway bridge in Scotland.

But having crossed the broad Mississippi into the State of Illinois, some very intricate route navigation had to be undertaken in order reach the city of Edwardsville. Finding Edwardsville was the key to our finding the correct alignment of Route 66 route through Illinois. When we eventually arrived there, Edwardsville proved to be a handsome city of more than twenty thousand souls, with an attractive old-time downtown commercial area and a proud history of raising governors of the State of Illinois. But never, not even once, did we see a sign for, or any hint of the existence of, Edwardsville before we actually entered the city. The authorities were clearly determined that Edwardsville should be a well kept secret from the outside world, in case anyone came and spoiled it.

This failure was obviously a solitary aberration, because for the remainder of the journey through Illinois, the highway authorities excelled themselves. Direction signs were provided in an exemplary fashion, and the old Route 66 was marked impeccably. At various points the course of the old route had varied over the years as new sections were opened and realignments of the highway implemented. Each of the various sections was clearly identified and designated with the era in which it had served as the historic highway, for example 1926-1930, or 1930-1938. Well done Illinois, and take note other States!

Credit for this might also have been due to an active and enthusiastic Illinois Route 66 Association. Certainly Illinois had taken its Route 66 history to heart, and had the money and the resources to do something about it. The old route was peppered with heritage sites recalling its heyday. There were lovingly restored 1930s filling stations, old diners reopened as museums, and eccentric roadside curios like the Gemini Giant, an enormous fibreglass astronaut holding a rocket which towered over Wilmington. For some of the small towns along the old route, jumping on the Old Route 66 bandwagon had been a life line in terms of jump starting economic revival and restoring a measure of civic pride.

The State of Illinois itself was a pleasant surprise. Far from being industrial and heavily populated as we had expected, we found ourselves jogging leisurely through small towns and villages of elegant houses, manicured lawns and well-kept frontages, clustered round short Main Streets of flat-fronted 1900s stores with canopied boardwalks. Some villages had attractive town centre squares – the equivalent of the good old English village green – and there were no abandoned car wrecks to be seen. Fertile farmland, a mixture of arable and dairy farms, separated the communities. All looked well in Illinois, the Land of Lincoln, and our destination for the night was Springfield, the state capital and home of the State Capitol.

Chapter 11

Springfield shared its name with eight other US cities of the same name, all of them in different States. We had already encountered Springfield, Missouri. Anyone wanting to collect the full set would also have to visit Colorado, Tennessee, Virginia, Vermont, Massachusetts, Ohio and Oregon. Now America is a splendidly varied country with a wealth of diverse cultures and subcultures, and everyone knows that America is the land of choice. Choosing a salad dressing – yes, that old litany once again of blue cheese, ranch, Italian, French, or thousand island – or even a bread roll – will that be rye, pumpernickel, sourdough, multigrain or wholemeal, with poppy or sesame seeds? – required serious decision making. But paradoxically, America was also singularly conformist and homogenous, especially when it came to names. Every State seemed to have a Madison County and a city called Lebanon (as well as Springfield). Every downtown had its First, Second, Third and Fourth Street, which intersected with Jackson, Polk, Jefferson and Lincoln Avenue. Just a few blocks away from the downtown area came Chestnut, Walnut, Oak and Sequoia Avenue. Really daring communities sometimes replaced these with

Georgia, Virginia, Massachusetts and Delaware. And access to the city from the freeway was usually along Brandywine Boulevard. The pattern never varied. It was probably laid down in the American constitution and zealously guarded by a succession of Chief Justices.

We learned that Springfield, Illinois, was famous for its association with two great benefactors of the American nation, Abraham Lincoln and Ed Waldmire. Abraham Lincoln was an obscure country lawyer who made the big time, and Ed Waldmire was the world renowned inventor of the Cozy Dog. It was a cause for mild disappointment that we failed to locate the 'Cozy Dog Drive-In' on the southern outskirts of Springfield, probably due to the fact that the one-way system of roads in the city centre meant that north bound and south bound travellers on Route 66 entered and left the city on different streets. Ed apparently invented the Cozy Dog in the early 1940s and, according to the Route 66 video which we had watched, this invention was responsible single-handedly for powering the American economy to new levels of productivity and maintaining America's industrial supremacy. The Cozy Dog is basically a hot dog without the bun, a batter-coated frankfurter on a stick. The productivity theory was that the eater could eat the Cozy Dog with one hand, which still left the other hand free to continue with such patriotic duties as operating a blast furnace, performing brain surgery or driving a railway locomotive. America also owed a debt of gratitude to Ed's wife, clearly a marketing genius in her own right, who had firmly vetoed the product's original name, the Crusty Cur. We were sorry we had missed out on visiting Ed's historic restaurant – named 'Best Landmark in Illinois' in a 2002 magazine - and decided to concentrate on Abraham Lincoln.

We parked the Pontiac in Springfield's downtown area and became real tourists for a while. Not surprisingly, the story and personality of Abraham Lincoln dominated the town. Although he was born in a log cabin in the state of Tennessee, it is with Springfield that Lincoln will always associated. He practiced here as a provincial lawyer, he raised his family here, he served in the local Illinois legislature and he lived here in the only house that he ever owned.

And it was from Springfield that he embarked on his final journey to Washington, saying goodbye to his friends and neighbours in his emotional Farewell Address at the town railroad station on the eleventh of February 1861. "My friends, no one, not in my situation, can appreciate my feeling of sadness at this parting. To this place, and the kindness of these people, I owe everything. Here I have lived a quarter of a century, and have passed from a young to an old man. Here my children have been born, and one is buried. I now leave, not knowing when, or whether ever, I may return, with a task before me greater than that which rested upon Washington. Without the assistance of the Divine Being who ever attended him, I cannot succeed. With that assistance I cannot fail. Trusting in Him who can go with me, and remain with you, and be everywhere for good, let us confidently hope that all will yet be well. To His care commending you, as I hope in your prayers you will commend me, I bid you an affectionate farewell." He never returned to Springfield.

We toured Abraham's home, a modest two storey suburban home which he bought as a single storey dwelling and extended as his family grew, learned more about the Lincoln legend at the visitor centre, and photographed the historic Capitol Building of the State of Illinois where the great man cut his political teeth. His place in America's pantheon of secular saints seemed unassailable.

A quick scan through the Springfield City Guide confirmed the dominance of the cultural landscape exercised by the Lincoln heritage. Other visitor attractions offered by the city included the Lincoln Library, the Lincoln Law Office, the Lincoln Depot, the Lincoln Pew, the Lincoln Ledger, the Lincoln Tomb and the Lincoln Memorial Garden. Had we been making our visit week later, we could have tossed the caber and downed a wee dram at Springfield's annual Highland Games, no doubt held in honour of the President's Scottish connections. The Museum of Funeral Customs offered almost the only respite from the Lincoln saga. From its description, it seemed like a fun place for a visit, portraying in a user-friendly fashion the history of American funeral, grief and mourning customs, with a re-created embalming room with caskets, instruments and equipment. But even this cheerful place had succumbed to local expectation and showcased a full-sized reproduction of Lincoln's coffin.

By now it was late on Sunday afternoon and the city was virtually deserted, an excellent time for a swift walking tour. The downtown area was like the Marie Celeste. Somewhere close by, out of sight, a succession of railroad trains traversed the city centre at walking pace along unprotected tracks and across ungated crossings. The powerful and penetrating sound of their high-pressure air-horns swirled around the concrete canyons of the business district, their mournful wailing ebbing and flowing in a continuous rendition of a moose in labour. Since our nocturnal experience with the trains of the Santa Fé Railroad in Arizona a week before, I had seen an article in USA Today about the strength of feeling being generated in bedroom America by this noise.

The spectral wail of the American locomotive horn had long been associated in the national consciousness with the romance of distant places, of hopeful journeys, of lonely travellers in the night and the westward advance of progress. But the present reality had more to do with broken nights, disturbed sleep patterns and communities on the warpath. Instructed by safety regulations framed during an earlier era, American locomotive engineers traditionally had itchy trigger fingers, and believed it their civic duty to approach crossings with all sirens blazing, night and day.

In response to a growing crescendo of noise complaints, more than two thousand 'quiet zones' in twenty four states had been authorised. But now the protagonists of these 'quiet zones', where trains had been obliged to pass silently through intersections without sounding their horns except in an emergency, appeared to have lost their struggle for peace. The Federal railroad authority had decided to abolish all 'quiet zones', except where the local community could afford to spend up to a hundred thousand dollars per crossing installing new safety equipment. Nine million Americans would be at the mercy of the hooters. One community, which had previously benefited from 'quiet zone' designations at its eighteen crossings which served twenty six trains per day, had calculated that it stood to be assaulted by over four thousand horn blasts a day. After just one disturbed night at Holbrook, Arizona, I could well understand the strength of feeling.

We spent that night at a motel on the northern fringe of Springfield. Sunday evening was coming to a close, and the television religious programming had reached the other end of the denominational spectrum. Mother Angelica and her Sisters were praying the Rosary. "Holy Mary, pray for us now and in the hour of our deaths." The service was repetitive and the Sisters were persistent. Time after time after time, the Sisters intoned, "Holy Mary, pray for us now and in the hour of our deaths." And on this cheerful note, we turned in for the night.

Next morning, we left Springfield early. It was to be our last day driving the Pontiac and we were anxious to arrive in Chicago in good time and in style. As if sensing an imminent parting of the ways, the old vehicle seemed strangely reluctant to start this morning. After a prolonged period of apathetic churning, the motor eventually coughed into life and we eased away from the motel forecourt. The sky was blue and the old Route 66 was in fine fettle. We glided passed fields and woods, farmsteads and barnyards, horses and cattle. With the top down once more, we were open to the gentle elements of sun and breeze.

Far away to the left we could see the Interstate highway, with its non-stop procession of trucks and cars, and appreciated the calm and serenity of travelling in the style of yesteryear. Small town Illinois unrolled under our wheels. Elkhart, with its short Main Street and line of American flags, nestling behind the grain elevators across the railroad track; Broadwell, where the Pig Hip Restaurant, famous (well, famous in Illinois that is) for its Pig Hip Sandwiches between 1937 and 1991, has now been transformed into a museum; Atlanta, home of a two story high fibreglass giant carrying a hotdog.

Between towns, the Illinois landscape was gently rolling woodland. At Funks Grove, we spotted a sign for the sale of maple sirup (sic), and pulled off the highway and up the track to the old farm house. Small birds darted among the leafy trees and cornflower blue flowers speckled the grassy carpet beneath the trees. We were welcomed warmly by the mother of the present owner of the business and asked to mark our home town on the map of the world in their sirup store. Visitors from all over the world called at their store. Earlier in the year, a young man from Paris passed through on roller blades, headed for Los Angeles. An eccentric English woman, walking from Chicago to California had passed through and purchased maple sirup. She had certainly survived the first sixty miles of her journey but there was no record as to whether she made the next two thousand miles!

Mrs Funk and her husband had started producing maple sirup here in 1947. No, this wasn't a spelling mistake, we were told, as in the early days syrup was always spelled with an 'i' rather than a 'y'. The farm was on the site settled in 1824 by her husband's great grandfather, Isaac Funk. Isaac, who was a friend and fellow Illinois Senator of Abraham Lincoln, had also produced maple sirup here in those early days. It was believed that some of the maple trees in the grove were around five hundred years old, and that Iroquois Indians had produced sirup here before him. As the warmer days of early spring caused the sap to rise in the maple trees, these Iroquois people would have made slashes in the bark of each tree trunk and drained the sap through hollow reeds into wooden containers.

The first European settlers used much the same time honoured process. The sap extracted from the trees looked and tasted much like sweet water, but boiling about forty gallons of the raw sap resulted in about one gallon of concentrated sirup. Further boiling of the sirup produced maple sugar. The "sugaring off" time, when the winter snows began to melt by day but the nights remained freezing, was an exciting social interlude in the rural calendar as generations of families marked the ingathering of the maple harvest and the imminent end of the harsh winter with celebrations and dances. But now, in the early twenty-first century, this operation was run as a business which produced eighteen hundred gallons of sirup a year from six thousand taps connected by a network of plastic pipes. The whole area seemed to be steeped in history. It was also an idyllic setting of great natural beauty and tranquillity.

We were approaching the City of Pontiac, and as our trusty vehicle which had carried us all the way from California was a 1974 Pontiac Grande Ville it went without question that we should make a stop and pay homage to its birthplace. We were looking forward to seeing the vast Pontiac auto factory, and perhaps going on the visitor tour of the historic assembly plant. Even our Pontiac, which had started the day so reluctantly, seemed to perk up as if it recognized the place as we turned off Route 66 towards the centre of town. The City of Pontiac was a pretty town with a quiet and genteel central square lined with shops and commercial properties. At the centre of the square stood the County Court House, tall and elegant, with a classical white-columned portico bolted onto a soaring central tower in a style reminiscent of a French chateau.

We parked in the town square and set out to explore Pontiac. It was a surprise, and a big disappointment, to discover that the city had no connection whatsoever with the cars of the same name. They just both happened to have been named after the same Indian chief. The only engineering claim to fame of Pontiac was that it was a city of three swing bridges over the local river. Occasionally one of these bridges would swing open. That was about as exciting as it got in Pontiac.

As we drove out of Pontiac heading north, we spied the Old Log Cabin Restaurant, set slightly back from the road. This establishment had at one time (so we had read) been bodily repositioned to a different orientation when a realignment of the old Route 66 had been made. It seemed like an interesting story, and it was coffee time, so in we went. Inside, the lighting was rather subdued as indeed was whole atmosphere of the establishment, and we sat ourselves down on high stools at the old fashioned counter facing the chilled drinks cabinet and the rows of glasses. A number of elderly good ol' boys in baseball caps sat quietly at tables by themselves, drinking coffee and ordering lunchtime meals. The scenario was clear: 'her indoors who must be obeyed' was either running a quilting bee or cleaning house. He had been banished down to the café.

We had placed our order for coffee and cinnamon rolls when another customer, who happened to be a member of the local Friends of Route 66 organisation, came across to talk to us. The presence of such exotic foreign visitors on a charitable mission spurred her into action. The proprietor of the restaurant was summoned to photograph us as a record for posterity and to inscribe our names in the guest book. The phone wires between the Old Log Cabin Restaurant and the City of Pontiac began to hum, and we were informed that certain civic dignitaries would be hurrying out from the city to interview us.

Soon the city's Director of Tourism arrived to greet us. She was Betty, a friendly lady of around sixty, who shook our hands and formally welcomed us to Pontiac on behalf of her fellow citizens. Betty was most apologetic for having come alone. She had invited the editor of the local 'Pontiac Leader' to meet us, but unfortunately he was already hard up against his publishing deadline. The local radio reporter would definitely have come down to the Old Log Cabin to interview us, but he was in court to cover the crucial stage of a dramatic murder trial. A body had been found floating in the local river at Pontiac, deposited there, so it was alleged, by Chicago gangsters. All in all, it seemed that we were only the second most interesting thing happening in Pontiac that day.

Betty did a good job of selling the City of Pontiac to us, telling us about the three swing bridges and the building which had recently been acquired to house the Route 66 Hall of Fame. She kindly presented us with souvenir mugs and other keepsakes of our visit. And we promised we would tell other potential tourists about the charms of Pontiac, whilst making no promises about attracting inward investment by manufacturers of tractors or semiconductors.

We left the Old Log Cabin in the early afternoon sunshine, with top down and the wind blowing through our hair. This would be our final topless swansong and we would soon be within shouting distance of Chicago. We felt good, and the sweet smell of success was in our nostrils.

But success and failure tend to be close companions. Shortly after half past two, we made a routine stop to fill up with gasoline at Romeoville, an attractively named community at the fringes of the sprawling Chicago conurbation. As we pulled away from the filling station and onto the busy highway, unexpected disaster struck. The Pontiac just couldn't accelerate, it wouldn't pull away, in fact it would no longer go any faster than about five miles per hour. Waves of heavy trucks bore down on us threateningly. We turned into a side street to take stock of this new situation, and peered vainly under the hood for any clue as to what might be the problem. Nothing was visibly amiss. We drove cautiously up and down the street a couple of times, but the automatic transmission stubbornly refused to move out of bottom gear. We fought the inevitable conclusion for several minutes before accepting that there was no option but to walk back to the filling station and summon a mechanic with a tow truck.

Within half an hour, our beautiful Pontiac, blushing a deeper shade of blue and mortified with embarrassment, submitted to the indignity of having her front wheels hoisted off the road and being dragged ignominiously to Bob and Tod's Auto Care at Bolingbroke. Tod, the friendly tow truck driver, introduced us to half his family and gave us an account of his business career, but the personal touch and his caring bedside manner couldn't soften the awful blow of Tod's preliminary diagnosis – terminal failure of the automatic transmission system. It looked ominously like the end of the road for the Pontiac.

Bob and Tod's Auto Care couldn't deal with such serious problems, so Tod towed us a further couple of blocks to a garage which specialized in transmission problems. It was now four thirty in the afternoon. But they couldn't look at the vehicle until the next day, and couldn't even start to work on it until the day after that. The only option open to us was reluctantly to abandon the Pontiac to their tender mercies, and order up a rental car from the Hertz office just down the street. We were within twenty five miles of our destination, the Michigan lakeside at Chicago.

The bitterness of defeat was hard to take, and my inclination was to go away and crawl under a stone, or at least to drive straight to the hotel we had booked in Des Plaines, close Chicago's O'Hare Airport, and hide away. But Lois was made of stronger stuff, and she insisted that we should press on, battle Chicago's rush hour traffic and finish the course today. Quitting was not an option. My face dropped at the thought of the futility of such a pointless gesture, but a moment's reflection persuaded me that she was right, as usual!

So it was that an hour later, we drove down Chicago's Jackson Boulevard, passed the 'End of Historic Route 66' sign and turned along the lakeside drive beside Lake Michigan. But our hour of triumph had been turned into a moment of anticlimax and pathos, our sense of accomplishment was somewhat muted. After an epic journey of almost three thousand miles, we breasted the finishing tape, not in a magnificent example of Detroit's ultimate motoring machine, to the admiring glances of the watching citizens, but unnoticed and unacclaimed, in a rented Mitsubishi!

Checking in at Pontiac, Illinois

Burger giant, Atlanta, Illinois

As good as new, in Illinois

Still on the trail in Illinois

Route 66, by the shores of Lake Michigan, Chicago

Kick-off chez Krispy Kreme's, Andrew and Christine

Biltmore, North Carolina, not Palace of Versailles or château by the Loire

Skyline Drive, Shenandoah National Park, Virginia

Chapter 12

Lois had been to Chicago before, but this was my first visit to the windy city by the great lake. And it proved to be a great place for a few days rest and recreation after twelve solid days on the road. We visited dear friends with whom a reunion was long overdue. We strolled by the shore of Lake Michigan and wandered along historic Navy Pier. We took a good fix of culture by visiting the Art Institute, a splendid art gallery with corridors and halls filled with American and European paintings and with European porcelain (a weakness of mine). We ate enormously decadent ice cream sundaes at Ghirardelli's. We rode the 'loop' suburban trains. We sought out the best coffee shops and delis. And we soared a quarter of a mile into the sky to the top of the Sears Tower, the tallest building in America. On this clear and sunny day, the vistas across city and lake were spectacular.

The Sears Tower was completed in 1973, and at 1450 feet it held the undisputed title of 'Highest Building in the World' for twenty three years. The proverbial spanner was suddenly thrown into the works in 1996 when the twin Petronas Towers in Malaysia were unveiled, claiming to be thirty three feet higher than the Sears Tower, although they had twenty two fewer stories. An emergency meeting of the Council on Tall Buildings and Urban Habitat was convened. (No, I didn't make this up. This august body really does exist.) Exercising the wisdom of Solomon, the Council agreed on four categories of measurement for tall buildings, which were: height to the structural top; height to the highest occupied floor; height to the top of the roof; height to the top of antenna. The Sears Tower led the world in categories two and three. But the Malaysian twin towers had sneaked their way to the honours in the first category, thanks to their 111-foot decorative spires. Dignified in defeat, the Sears Tower had no plans to add its own spires.

The published tariff for visitors to ascend to the Sears Towers viewing area was $9-95. It sounded a reasonable price to visit the tallest building in America, and as there were two of us I handed over a $20 bill. Even I could calculate that the change would be ten cents. I was wrong of course. The total charge was $21.89 – I had forgotten the inevitable sales taxes. I handed over a further $10 bill and walked away with yet another fistful of small change to add to the ballast already weighing me down. To foreign visitors it seemed amazing that Americans hadn't long since insisted on transparent tax-inclusive pricing. Whatever the item we purchased, the price at the point of sale always came as a complete surprise, and only a mathematical genius could be sure of proffering the right money. Here's a real live example to exercise the brain cells. Take an item sold in a store at Bellwood, Illinois, priced at $8.75. Now add the city sales tax at 1%, the county sales tax at 1.5% and the State sales tax at 6.25%, and don't forget that all tax rates vary by city and by county, and are subject to change on January 1 and July 1. The price to be paid of course came to $9.51½. It's on a par with another American money matter which puzzles and confuses visitors; why do bills of all dollar denominations have to be the same size and the same shade of green?

Three days after we arrived in Chicago, Andrew and his team flew in from London, keen to get their project underway. The press conference and kick-off meeting was scheduled for early the next morning. A whole raft of functions and appointments were in their daily calendar for the next two weeks and the team was raring to hit the old two lane highway bound for California. The only person who was missing was the star of the show, the vast and venerable Pontiac, ignominiously penned in a workshop compound at Bolingbroke in the outer suburbs of Chicago.

We had kept in touch daily with the chief mechanic to monitor progress, and Andrew and I made a visit to check out how the patient was progressing. I was a little anxious because this was to be Andrew's first sight of her, the vehicle he had bought without ever having seen, and our stewardship of her had not exactly ended covered in roses. But happily it was love at first sight, and Andrew's heart was won over by the sight of a beautiful lady laid low. Our discussion with Gordon was also reassuring. Gordon had been working long hours, evenings included (his family were beginning to complain that they never saw him anymore), to get the vehicle back on the road, and he was confident enough to promise us that the car would be ready by the next afternoon. If he could deliver on this, at least Andrew and team would be able to set out on the correct day as scheduled, albeit six or seven hours later than planned.

The technical report on our long suffering Pontiac went something like this. The bottom line of the problem was that the automatic transmission system had suffered total failure and a piston had broken. The solution was very labour intensive, and as far as I could understand involved taking the motor apart, stripping down the automatic transmission system, welding the broken piston, cleaning the insides of the system and the pistons, replacing various seals, and putting it all back together again. It was a painstaking task that couldn't be hurried. The reasons behind the failure were scary. Someone had poured brake fluid into the transmission system, perhaps a couple of years ago or even more. Gordon's explanation of the rationale behind this was that it was a dodge sometimes used by auto engineers as a temporary fix when the transmission system developed a leak. The brake fluid set up a chemical reaction with the rubber seals, causing them to swell and so temporarily plugged the leak. But the chemical reaction with the seals continued, and eventually the seals broke up, resulting in transmission failure and a broken piston. It had been a failure waiting to happen. We had driven halfway across a continent before the inevitable day of reckoning arrived. Thanks to the various ministrations of Vince and Hal, we'd made a safe arrival in Chicago, but only just!

The next morning dawned wet and windy. It was to be the day we hit the road again, continuing on across America towards the Atlantic seaboard. Having relinquished responsibility for the faithful old Pontiac which had brought us so far, we were planning to head for the east coast by rental car, taking a looping trajectory to the south and the east via the state of Tennessee before heading north and east towards Washington DC. But first there was the press launch of Andrew's charity drive to attend before we could draw a line under the first half of our coast-to-coast journey and start the second half.

In the early morning rain, we navigated with some difficulty through heavy traffic to the Krispy Kreme Doughnut restaurant, tucked away behind the main runway of Chicago's O'Hare Airport in the suburb of Elk Grove. Despite the miserable weather, it was an occasion when the inherent goodness of American people shone like a beacon, bright and clear. The warm and welcoming folk of the local ALS support group, several families of them, turned out to greet us at the unholy hour of seven thirty in the morning. The Krispy Kreme corporation had sent along their historic liveried 1938 Chevrolet delivery truck. Our host was Kevin, the company's friendly local manager, who kindly made available the hospitality area of the restaurant and generously provided an unlimited supply of coffee and doughnuts. Reporters and photographers of both the local Pioneer Press and the Chicago Tribune had braved the elements to photograph the event for their readers and to interview the intrepid English travellers. Unsuspecting early morning customers stopping by to collect their breakfast doughnuts were jolted into wakefulness by an impromptu burst of song from the assembled Silver Minstrels. And a rousing motivational send-off speech was delivered by James P Petri, Trustee of the City of Elk Grove, on behalf of the mayor and the local community.

We eventually took our leave of these good folk, fortified by their kindness and hospitality and by a generous intake of doughnuts. The doughnuts were, in fact, a revelation! Light and fresh, in various flavours and with a range of fillings, they literally melted in the mouth, a far cry from our preconception of stodgy jam-filled confections with the emphasis on the word dough. Diplomatically, we asked no questions about carbohydrates and cholesterol. The Krispy Kreme Corporation itself was as impressive as its doughnuts. Founded in 1937 and now making three million doughnuts per day, it was proud of its long track record of working with local communities and supporting charities. The gist of its standard fundraising deal was that doughnuts were sold in bulk to charities and non-profit organizations, which then raised funds by selling them to supporters at the retail price. Obviously this was a clever marketing tactic by Krispy Kreme, as it gave them another wholesale sales channel as well as considerable social kudos. But it certainly seemed to be a model of a modern socially aware company. And I'm not too easily impressed, and neither do I have a vested interest. I'm not even a shareholder, although I confess to having checked them out. We left with the zeal of new converts, and also with a copious supply of complimentary doughnuts, half a dozen boxes which each contained a dozen nutritious doughnuts. For the next few days these kept the wolf from the door as we headed east, and provided sustaining coffee break snacks for Gordon and his team of mechanics at Bolingbroke.

We said our goodbyes to our friends who would later set out for Los Angeles in the Pontiac, fortified with doughnuts for their west-bound drive along Route 66. Our three days of being confined to one city had fired our appetite for the open road once more, and we enthusiastically launched ourselves on the network of urban freeways and expressways which facilitated our speedy getaway from the greater Chicago area.

Chicago is a great city which has contributed so much to the industrial and economic development of America. One of its lesser known gifts to America – to the world, even – is the McDonalds Corporation. Out of respect for the company which had sustained us in some of the remotest parts of the American West, we felt just a twinge of regret that we hadn't visited the location of the very first McDonalds restaurant, now reopened as a visitor attraction, museum and historic site in Des Plaines, no less. In 1954 Ray Kroc, an entrepreneurial salesman and distributor of a patented milk shake mixer, heard about Dick and Mac McDonald's hamburger stand in San Bernardino, California, which had bought eight of his milk shake machines. He persuaded the two brothers that it would be a good business idea to open a chain of restaurants based on their methods, mainly because he thought he would be able to sell eight of his milk shake machines to each one. "Who could we get to open them for us?" Dick McDonald asked. "Well," Kroc answered, "what about me?" And the rest is history, as they say.

Neither did we get to visit that distinguished educational establishment Hamburger University, originally founded in Elk Grove in 1961 but since relocated to a landscaped hundred acre campus in the neighbouring suburb of Oak Brook. It might not be as prestigious as Yale and Harvard, but it has sixteen resident professors, teaches students from more than a hundred countries, claims to have overtaken the US Army as America's largest training organization, and has graduated over seventy thousand McDonald's managers. But there was no sign of Doughnut University, or of the Krispy Kreme Business School either, which clearly amounted to an A-minus in social responsibility for the Krispy Kreme Corporation.

We were relishing the prospect of a day of fast Interstate motoring, behind the wheel of a new and sensible sized rental car, not the majestic but ponderous thirty year old Pontiac. Once released from the spider's web of highways of the Chicago conurbation, we flew like a bird let loose, like a greyhound from the trap, like a bat out of hell. Middle America unrolled like a film in fast forward during a day in which we travelled through four states; Illinois, Indiana, Ohio and Kentucky.

At the southern end of Lake Michigan, the elevated freeway pierced the industrial heart of the town of Gary, Indiana, a place unlikely to win any awards for beauty and charm. Gary was the steel capital of America, and came complete with attractive vistas of steel mills, coke ovens, blast furnaces, smoke stacks, stock yards, railroad depots, bridges, iron ore docks and coal heaps. Heading southwards, the wide, flat and featureless farming landscape of central Indiana gave way to the pleasant rolling country of homesteads, hamlets and farms of southern Indiana. We caught glimpses of the high buildings of downtown Indianapolis as we looped round the city beltway, Indy 500 style, before emerging like a sling shot on a trajectory towards Ohio. We threaded the beautifully wooded valleys of south western Ohio and tangled briefly with the early evening rush hour traffic of Cincinnati, a city which Winston Churchill once described as "one of the most beautiful of America's inland cities." We were a little surprised that so many office staff seemed to be knocking off work so early in the afternoon, even for a Friday, until we realised that as we entered Ohio we had crossed into a new time zone.

We left Cincinnati by the very distinctive Roebling Suspension Bridge, which had been a remarkable visual symbol of the city since it was opened in 1866. By the standards of the American Midwest that was seriously old, and yet it still carried thousands of vehicles high over the Ohio River every day. Thanks to a collision on the bridge between a couple of motorists rather too keen to start their week-ends, we had plenty of time to enjoy the panoramic views up and down the river. The Ohio River was the State border, and we crossed the suspension bridge from Cincinnati directly into the Kentucky community of Covington.

Before the Civil War, Kentucky had been a 'slave state', whereas Ohio had been a 'free state'. The controversial notion of building the bridge had been opposed by some on both sides who thought it would encourage an influx of runaway slaves. But it was favoured by some Kentucky farmers who thought it would enable them to sell their agricultural products in the big city, and opposed by Ohio farmers who feared the competition from Kentucky farmers. Its construction took over ten years, interrupted by shortages of cash and by the Civil War, and when completed in December 1866 it was the longest suspension bridge in the world, with a main span of 1057 feet. The suspension wires were specially imported from England. For those with an interest in technology, its promotional material made the claim that it was 'the first bridge to utilize both vertical suspenders and diagonal stays', design features it probably had in common with certain items of underwear of the period. Cincinnati's Roebling Suspension Bridge held its record for a mere three years until the 211 feet longer Niagara Falls Suspension Bridge in New York State was opened.

We continued south through the beautiful sun-drenched Kentucky countryside, the undulating highway winding its way between grassy hills and woods. This was 'bluegrass' country, but to us everything was green, wonderfully green. Everything had that freshly laundered look. Green hills, green trees, green fields around us, clear blue sky above. Elegant horses grazed in white fenced compounds. Neat white farmsteads dotted the hillsides and peeped demurely through the trees. Kentucky looked idyllic. A local preacher once described heaven to his congregation as "a Kentucky of a place." It seemed to make sense.

But Kentucky wasn't always so tranquil. As a slave state, it would have been expected to cast in its lot with the rebel

South during the Civil War. But Kentucky was a community divided against itself, and local militia were raised to fight on both sides, the North and the South. Early in the conflict, a bloody and decisive battle at Perryville forced the Confederate supporters to withdraw, leaving Kentucky in Union hands for the rest of the Civil War.

Chapter 13

We spent the night at Berea, a small country town in the centre of the state, which billed itself the 'Folk Arts and Crafts Capital of Kentucky'. Berea modestly reckoned to offer its visitors 'a graceful blend of southern hospitality and Appalachian tradition'. Next morning, which was Saturday, we took a stroll round town. The ladies of the local Mennonite community were running a home bake sale, but otherwise the town's arts and crafts claim was looking a bit thin. The municipal publicity material forgot to mention that the town had taken its name from northern Greek city of Berea between Thessalonica and Athens, now known as Verria, which was praised in the Book of Acts for the noble character of its citizens. It was a strange omission, as the history of Berea Kentucky recorded some pretty noble citizens of its own.

The real story in Berea proved to be Berea College. Much of the town was campus territory, and the elegant college buildings, some with dignified columned frontages, stood on gracious lawns among tall leafy trees. The college had a fascinating and honourable history which in some way was a cameo of the social and political tensions which were endemic to pre-Civil War Kentucky, as a southern 'slave state' with a northern border with 'free' Ohio. Berea College was founded on anti-slavery principles in 1855 by the Rev. John Fee, an ardent abolitionist, with the radical vision of a community committed to interracial education and with the financial backing of a rich benefactor called Cassius M. Clay. It was the only integrated college in the South for forty years, and its dormitory buildings stood alternately black, white, black, and so on. But it very soon fell foul of segregationalist legislation, and rather than compromise its principles, the College closed its doors in 1859 until the end of the Civil War six years later. After the war, many of its new students were freed slaves and African-American former soldiers of the Union Army. To this day, as a liberal arts college, it had provided scholarships to all students who needed one, in return for work done for the college on campus.

We continued south, the highway threading its way between hills clad with trees of every shade of green, both deciduous trees and evergreens. The colours were luminous under the bright sun and the clear blue sky, and we were missing the freedom of the open top motoring to which we had become accustomed. At Corbin we left the main highway, attracted by a sign to Sanders Court Motel and Café. After all, this was Kentucky, and the opportunity to visit the original Kentucky Fried Chicken restaurant was something we just couldn't pass up. As it was with most of the legendary American entrepreneurs, the Colonel Sanders story was an interesting combination of business flair and chance opportunity. The Colonel – and there seemed to be some doubt as to whether he was a real Colonel or the holder of an honorary rank in a local militia force – had pursued a variety of different careers but by the late 1930s he was operating a motel and café in the small town of Corbin. He was famous in the neighbourhood for his Country Ham Breakfast, but the business threatened to go into sudden decline in the early 1950s when the highway authorities decided to construct the Interstate highway and a local bypass. So at the ripe young age of sixty six, Sanders took the recipe for fried chicken which he had perfected in his kitchen and hawked it round to other café owners. He generated enough business interest to create his franchise business in 1956. His secret recipe involving eleven herbs and spices is a trade secret to this day, but the rest, to use the time worn phrase again, is history.

The original café was now inevitably a heritage centre and museum, but it was also still in business as a KFC outlet. With dutiful reverence, we peered into the homely 1940s kitchen where the Colonel had experimented with his pressure frying techniques, and inspected the simple décor and fittings of a sample motel room. The old Colonel was clearly a student of family psychology. He had a theory that families wouldn't stay at a motel unless the lady of the house had first checked out the accommodation, so he incorporated a sample room in his café so that she could see it in advance and know exactly what to expect. It was a simple but effective selling tool, and indicative of the customer service ethos and 'no nasty surprises' philosophy which he built into his future restaurant chain.

But today the late Colonel's business empire was losing ground, struggling against a tide of saturated fats and consumer fears of frying. So what was the future direction of KFC? In an attempt to clarify its strategy, the company's marketing chief explained helpfully, "KFC isn't coming out of left field. Our food evolution is a steady part of a bigger picture". This choice example of marketing speak didn't cut the bacon for me. Perhaps the time was ripe for the return of the Kentucky Country Ham 'finger lickin' good' Breakfast!

At Corbin, signposts indicated the direction to the Cumberland Gap, fifty miles away to the south east. I had only the haziest of notions of what the Cumberland Gap might be, but it was certainly a celebrated location, made famous in England by an irreverent popular song sung by Lonnie Donegan, half a century ago. The catchy tune began to swirl around in the head.

> "Fifteen miles on the Cumberland Gap, fifteen miles on the Cumberland Gap,
> I've got a girl, six feet tall, sleeps in the kitchen with her feet in the hall,
> Fifteen miles on the Cumberland Gap.
> Two old ladies sitting on the sand, each one wishing the other was a man,
> Fifteen miles on the Cumberland Gap."

These lyrics intensified the sense of mystery and give absolutely no clue as to what there might be to see at the Cumberland Gap. The temptation to turn aside from the planned itinerary and find out was strong. What had happened to the girl and the two old ladies? Would the historic kitchen and hall now be a heritage centre and museum? Unfortunately we would never know. Our tight schedule meant that we must continue south to the State of Tennessee. But research (and some helpful National Park literature) helped us to fill in the knowledge gaps.

First discovered by Europeans in the latter half of the eighteenth century, the Cumberland Gap has assumed a romantic position in American folklore, both for its spectacular views and the beauty of its sun gilded mountain tops, and for its role as a crucial gateway to the exploration and settlement of the American West. The Gap is located where the borders of Tennessee, Kentucky and Virginia meet, and it constitutes a major gap in the forbidding Appalachian Mountains chain which had corralled early settlement into the eastern seaboard of the continent. By the year 1810, almost 300,000 settlers, men women and children, crossed the Gap into Kentucky. This influx of sturdy self reliant migrants from the east, rugged individualists, homesteaders and trades folk with no traditional ties to slavery, went a long way to explaining why Kentucky, a 'slave' state and member of the seceding Confederate States, proved to be a deeply divided house and reluctant rebel in the forthcoming Civil War.

We headed south from Corbin and crossed into eastern Tennessee. The geographical change from Kentucky was immediate. We had been travelling through a landscape of tree covered hills. The hills now became mountains. The highway curved upwards in a sweeping ramp until we were running at mountain top level, with commanding panoramic views and green forested vistas on all sides. In due course, the highway swept down from the sky, through the outskirts of the former state capital, Knoxville, and into the Central Valley of Tennessee. Splashes of colour from clusters of multi-hued poppies enlivened the highway embankments. Beside the road stood small groups of princess trees, an exotic import from China, now naturalized and widespread across Tennessee, North Carolina and Virginia. In contrast with the prevalent green vegetation, the dark timber skeletons of these leafless trees were dripping with clusters of bell shaped lilac flowers which, in a reversal of nature's normal sequence, bloomed before the leaves appeared.

In the far distance, way to the east, the Blue Ridge Mountains stood as a smoky grey smudge on the distant horizon.

Beside the highway, to the north and the south, green sub-Alpine meadows stepped away up the sides of the wide Central Valley towards the tree topped summits, like a piece of Bavaria in America. Everything seemed bright, clean and wholesome, the gentle reflection of the pale blue sky enhancing that newly minted look. The line of a song came to mind. "God's in his heaven, all's right with the world!" It was just the impression Tennessee gave.

But there was obviously more to Tennessee than appeared on the benign surface. In fact Tennessee had a turbulent roller coaster of a history. In the early days of European exploration, it had been the subject of a three way tussle between the Native Americans, the French and the British. It had successively been the western counties of the State of North Carolina, the breakaway State of Franklin, and the Southwest Territory of the federal government, before joining the Union as the State of Tennessee in 1796. Tension and conflict between the settlers and the Native American tribes culminated in 1838 in the shameful 'Trail of Tears', when the people of the Cherokee Nation were expelled en masse and dispatched on the long march to Indian Territory. At the time of the Civil War, Tennessee was finely balanced between pro-slavery and anti-slavery supporters and was the last of the secession states to elect to join the rebel Confederates. Many Tennessee citizens joined the Confederate Army, and many joined the Union Army. Battles raged across the State and widespread destruction ensued.

We passed a roadside billboard which advertised Ripley's 'Aquarium of the Smokies' at nearby Gatlinburg on the edge of the Great Smoky Mountains National Park. 'Vicious sharks. Satisfaction guaranteed. Money back if not satisfied.' It seemed like a fair offer, and it was tempting to turn aside just to test out the robustness of the satisfaction guarantee.

Just how vicious is vicious? What macabre demonstrations of viciousness would be on offer? How would I prove my dissatisfaction? Unfortunately it would all have to remain a mystery.

Our destination for the night was Johnson City, a pleasant community in the Tri-Cities area of Eastern Tennessee, where we had been invited to spend some time as guests of good friends. From here, we took a side excursion into North Carolina. Between Tennessee and North Carolina, the highway wound skywards again as it navigated through the Great Smoky Mountains, a southern appendix of the great Appalachian range. From our high vantage point, the clouds clinging to the hillside and carpeting the floor of the low valleys, and the steam and trails of damp mist rising from the trees after a sudden rainstorm gave graphic illustration of how the 'Smokies' got their name.

Our target in North Carolina was the Biltmore Estate, a splendidly opulent pile in the style of a French château built in the final years of the nineteenth century and set in a magnificent mountain parkland setting. Intended to rival the gracious country estates of Europe, it was designed for George Washington Vanderbilt by Richard Hunt, an American architect trained at the School of Fine Arts in Paris, and became the largest private residence in America. Hunt modelled his French Renaissance-style design on the great châteaux of the Loire Valley – Blois, Chenonceau and Chambord – and drew inspiration from his visits to the elegant estates of the English nobility at Knowle and Hatfield House. The latter, which incorporates the Royal Palace of Hatfield where England's Queen Elizabeth the First spend some of her childhood, was built almost four hundred years ago by Robert Cecil, Earl of Salisbury, and has been in the Cecil family ever since.

No expense was spared in the construction of the remarkable Biltmore edifice. Constructed by an imported army of toiling artisans, artists and labourers accommodated in a temporary village, the home showcased all the wonders of the latest technologies, Victorian style; central heating, electricity, elevators, plumbing and piped water, gymnasium and indoor swimming pool. It is doubtful the world had seen its like since King Solomon bowled over the Queen of Sheba with the splendour of his domestic arrangements and his temple building exploits two thousand years before. Sadly, Hunt died in the same year as his masterpiece was completed.

The result was a remarkably sympathetic union between conspicuous extravagance and homely domesticity. Ironically – and perhaps fittingly - the marriage in the following generation between Cornelia Vanderbilt of America's 'nouveau riche' industrialist Vanderbilt family and the Honourable John Cecil of Britain's ancient political Cecil dynasty, brought the Biltmore Estate into the ownership of a new generation of Cecils. The original William Cecil, the first Baron Burghley, Secretary of State and Lord High Treasurer to Queen Elizabeth the First in the sixteenth century, would have appreciated the irony.

This gracious residence was one of a number of distinctive features thrown up by our short stay in Tennessee and North Carolina, reminding us that we were now in the American 'South'. Elegant dining on grits and Charleston shrimps; a warning that we were committing a misdemeanour worthy of up to eleven months and twenty nine days imprisonment if we brought a gun into a place which served alcohol; working parties of convicts from the local correctional facility toiling beside the freeway, watched over by shotgun toting prison guards; the Billy Graham Parkway, named for a celebrated local resident near to the city of Asheville.

We left Tennessee with a sense that this was the final leg of an epic journey. Heading north up the main central valley of Tennessee towards the State of Virginia and jostling for road space with a growing volume of truck traffic, we were happy to drop off the freeway as soon as it was possible to do so and turn onto the Blue Ridge Parkway. This was a classic American trail, a winding traffic-free two lane switchback highway, riding the crest of the Blue Ridge Mountains for more than a hundred miles, weaving through ancient woodland and natural meadows, the domain of the reclusive barred owl, soaring hawks, giant butterflies, chattering chipmunks and American brown bears. Dramatic panoramas opened alternately to right and left. Pink azaleas beside the highway added their splashes of colour to the lilac cascades of the princess trees. Scattered between the trees, carpets of pale pink and blue spring flowers were beginning to burst through.

Far below and away to the west, the sinuous silver ribbon of the melodiously named Shenandoah River glinted in the sunlight in the distance. The wide views of hillsides and mountains were a palette of pastel shades, of greens, blues, mauves and browns, like an undiscovered masterpiece by Monet or one of his fellow French impressionists, as ranks of parallel ridges of the Appalachians intersected and overlapped until they merged with a hazy horizon. A sharp shower of rain was quickly followed by wispy tendrils of steam which clung to the firs and rose dreamily from the meadows. A furry brown bear cub bounded playfully up an embankment between the trees. A couple of deer stood in the centre of the highway, unselfconsciously drinking from puddles of water which had formed on the crown of the road, unconcerned by the traffic which cautiously eased past them.

Our target for the night was the historic junction town of Front Royal, lying in the northern Shenandoah Valley and strategically located at the confluence of a network of highways; from Pennsylvania to the north, from Washington to the east, and stretching away into Tennessee and Kentucky to the south and the west. The first tourist to discover this area was Johannes Lederer, a German doctor-explorer from Hamburg who in 1670 crossed the Blue Ridge Mountains from Maryland together with an English companion and a lone Indian guide and interpreter. The notes and sketches he took home must have been pretty persuasive, as the area soon became an attractive destination for European settlers.

For those settlers who arrived in the area in the late seventeenth century and the first half of the eighteenth century, French and Dutch fur trappers, German farmers, Scots-Irish lumberjacks and English Quakers, Front Royal was a staging post and gateway to the undiscovered west, and the meandering Shenandoah River was their highway both for advancing into the interior and for floating the harvest of oak timber downstream to the cities of Virginia and the Atlantic Ocean.

The town of Front Royal was formally founded later in the eighteenth century by French Huguenots, but soon came under British control. During the Civil War, Front Royal was on the front line, a place of violent death and destruction. In 1862, the town was captured after a dramatic march by the southern General 'Stonewall' Jackson who 'liberated' Front Royal from Union forces in a historic battle in which brother fought against brother. As war ebbed and flowed over the next three years, many properties in the area were ruined by the scorched earth policy of Union forces under General (later President) Ulysses S Grant.

Like every other American town, Front Royal had to be capital of something. Front Royal's self-appointed distinction was the modest 'Canoe Capital of Virginia'. For us, this genteel town with its gracious colonial ambiance was an easy fifty miles paddling distance to the Atlantic coast, to Washington's Dulles Airport and a flight home to Europe, a convenient staging post for leaving the country. It was a final opportunity for a light breakfast of buckwheat pancakes with seasonal berries and whipped cream, decorated with a generous helping of Canadian back bacon and anointed with Vermont maple syrup, imprisoned in a stockade of icing-sugar dusted French toast.

Incidentally, I once described the American delicacy of French toast to an incredulous Parisian – "mais non!" Not surprisingly, it's totally unknown in France! But confusion on matters of nourishment can work the other way too. Most Americans would be shocked to learn that filet Américain, a favourite of the burghers of Brussels, comes as a putrid heap of finely shredded raw beef mixed with pink mayonnaise, delicious in sandwiches and salads. It's all part of the hitherto unrecognised field of international food politics. A highlight of my business visits to California used to be breakfast of English muffins, a product not available in England. Belgian buns – doughy discs with a topping of icing sugar and a cherry – are not to be found in Belgium. Swiss rolls are not eaten in the country of the Alps. Italian pizza is essentially an American invention. French fries, a name bestowed in America, are not even French; extensive research has revealed that these are definitely a Belgian invention – invented by Mr Frits, no less, an entrepreneur who opened a stand selling Belgian frites in 1861. An honourable exception to this catalogue of dissembling is the Danish pastry, where the product in Denmark still excels.

But our epic journey across a continent was almost over. Before we dropped down from the Skyline Drive to peaceful Front Royal two thousand feet below, we briefly parked up beside the highway. The gentle slanting rays of the late afternoon sun filtered through the leafy canopy and bathed the woodland in luminous green and gold. Our gaze met that of an American brown bear, watching us sleepily from his lofty perch among the foliage of a tree a few yards from the road's edge. Draped over a sturdy branch, his four furry paws dangled loosely, swaying with a gentle lazy rhythm.

He knew nothing about our world and we knew little about his. He watched us with the confident relaxed assurance that comes from knowing that he was on home turf, in his own domain, and that we were the strangers. But there was plenty of room in his airy mountain-top world for both of us, and from his demeanour, it was clear that he was content to share it with us. And we were happy to think that he was adding his own welcome to those of the many special folk who had been so welcoming of us over the last three weeks, as we travelled across America, the wrong way.

Epilogue

Readers with an inquisitive streak will probably be asking whether the charity drive was a success and what happened to the Pontiac. Happily, Andrew and his team (together with the faithful Pontiac) arrived safely at their destination on the Pacific coast. True to type, the old vehicle kept them on their toes by introducing various random, but non-terminal, faults – gremlins in the lighting circuit in Arizona tripped the hazard warning lights into permanent operation and closed down the brake warning lights; at destination's end in California, half of the breaking system was found to have ceased to function. Thanks to the support and sponsorship of the Avis Corporation, who had generously provided a back-up vehicle, the team was never totally without wheels. Again true to type, the final lap of the Pontiac's home run up-country to Sacramento was a high-wire act. Literally in fact, as a discarded wire coat-hanger found by the roadside saved the day when the earth lead fell apart a few miles short of home base. Put on sale in Sacramento, it was several months before the Pontiac found a new owner and opened the next chapter in her career. Sadly, she has not been seen since.

Andrew and Christine are still working tirelessly on behalf of MND/ALS sufferers. Members of the Silver Minstrels are still savouring the memories of a job well done. The cheque (or check) from Governor Schwarzenegger hasn't yet arrived.

As a result of this project, enough money was raised to enable the launch of the Lorna Custerson Tribute Fund, established as a perpetual fund to lease and provide specially adapted beds for sufferers from MND/ALS.

Printed in the United Kingdom
by Lightning Source UK Ltd.
124656UK00001B/61/A